# Hand Spun Hope

Beth,
Many thanks for
all your help.
Enjoy!
Jody

# Hand Spun Hope

## Making a Difference in Rural South Africa

Judith Baker Miller

ISBN: 1519116020
ISBN 13: 9781519116024

dedicated to my mother,
Mary Jane Caveny Baker 1914-2006
She showed me what it looks like to join vision with action.

"Action without vision is only passing time,
vision without action is merely daydreaming,
but vision with action can change the world"

— Nelson Mandela

# Contents

# Introduction

perch on the ancient rocks at the top edge of the Blyde River Canyon looking out over the rough heights of the Drakensberg Mountains at the red-orange earth and the infinite shades of green in the bushveld below. All of my activity as a community developer over the last twelve years occurred within the wide view of this spot. The special thrum that is Africa vibrates within me. The persistent hum happens when bugs, bees, crickets, birds and wind all join together to form a life force that vibrates with immense vitality. The sun is strong and the sky encircling me is bright and clear, a startling blue. A bateleur eagle glides by riding the currents of wind in this immense canyon, the third largest in the world, and unlike the other two a green canyon teeming with life. The rocks are ancient, some 200 million years old, a number so unimaginably big it blows my mind wide open. And, if I consider the rock art sprinkled on the walls of the caves in this range, the spirit of the native, hunter-gatherer San people joins my party of one on the rock. I need to be touched by this primordial canyon's spacious wisdom to understand what really happened here in South Africa for me and for those with whom I worked.

When I arrived I was stripped down on many levels having just completed four rounds of dreaded and dreadful chemotherapy. I was thin, bald, weak and wobbly, but having a bout with cancer made me fighting mad and ready to stand up in a new way. I was determined to somehow make this world more of all I thought it should and could be. I'd been envisioning John Lennon's imagined world since my college days on the hippie-filled streets of Boston, and now was my chance to do what I could to make these ideals alive in the real world. It was time; this was my chosen ground for the action; and oh how I wanted to make a difference.

Despite my vulnerable state my ideals were shining bright, but the level of my ignorance was astounding. I had read books about the history of the country but was oblivious to the on-the-ground reality of tribes and cultures so very different from my own. A grid of invisible boundaries and barriers crawls across all the land visible from the top of the canyon. At first I didn't see them and when I began to trip on them I was both dismayed and confused. The essence of my story could be distilled down to all the times I bumped into, burst through and got bruised by the walls and ways of my newly adopted rainbow nation.

I would live in the land where Boer trekkers-- wandering Afrikaner farmers-- came in their sturdy wagons early in the 19th century when they had tired of the English rule down in the Cape. Before Nelson Mandela's 1994 election this area, the Transvaal province, was the epicenter of the Nationalist party which created and enforced the Apartheid system of racial separation for nearly fifty years. But I didn't understand what that would mean as I went between the grocery store in the white world of Hoedspruit and the long bank lines in the black world of Acornhoek. They were 30 miles apart physically and 30 million miles apart in most other ways.

I had no idea what it would be like to be a woman without a tribe in a land where tribes reign. Maybe, just maybe, that grand ignorance served me well. I often blundered across the borders without even seeing them, especially in the early days, and occasionally I crossed them with courage, wit, will or passion. In some cases I was beaten by these inflexible structures. Yet, from both the wins and the wrangles I gained a new strength.

I began my work with the six grandmothers of the Mapusha Weaving Cooperative in the rural outskirts of Acornhoek. And though I didn't know it then, empowerment was at the core of our work, theirs and mine. We were each and all-together struggling to stand up as women to some authority outside ourselves, willing ourselves not to shrink and not to bow.

I cheered for Regina———the cooperative's able chairwoman——— and cried with her as she wrestled to maintain her dignity in a fierce dispute with a Father of the church that had been the center of her life since childhood. She and the other women stood with me as I fought to hold the respect of the workers when I took on the daunting role of project manager to build their new studio. It was a particularly graceful coupling that brought us together just when I needed a cause to make me strong and when they needed support to stand up to the many bullies of their world.

These women were the warp in the tapestry we wove together. Their steady strength and willingness allowed me to be the weft, weaving in and through their lives with my fiery American-flavored ideas and initiatives. I came from a world of privilege and great freedom in comparison to their humble, rural lives. I had the good fortune to have a house I could sell to bankroll my idealistic longings, and parents with the means to catch me if I fell too hard.

They worried if there was enough mealie pap to get their families through the month and if the rains would come to bring their corn all the way to harvest. The babies of the younger women became the babies I was unable to bear myself, the children my children, and because I cared so deeply for all of them I had to grow bigger, speak louder, write more completely, fundraise more vigorously and do whatever else I could to improve their lives.

I was raised in the era when we threw off our bras and stopped shaving our legs. Having lived for the past two decades as a teacher and counselor in the liberal bubble of Portland, Oregon, I was cocky about my liberated self and snobbishly disdainful of the old fashioned, macho culture of South Africa. I thought it obvious that men and women were equals, yet, when I lived within this new world and watched women defer and silence themselves, I began to feel the many ways in which I, too, deferred to those I considered authorities and how I still let the fear of being revealed silence me too often. When I saw Emerencia————my wonderfully sassy apprentice————too ashamed to raise her eyes as she sat on the outskirts of a Hoedspruit gala, it hurt and it reawakened my own memories of being too scared to be seen, too scared something would awaken those wretched feelings of shame and humiliation.

When I asked the apprentices at the studio to make a drawing for me, they told me that only boys could draw. I remembered a painful pre-teen moment when I looked at my skewed drawing and labeled it bad, put down the pencil and stopped drawing for decades. Was it a similar self-judgement here with the girls of Rooiboklaagte? Did they believe they were inherently not good enough?

I've heard that we teach best what we most need to learn and if that is the case I tried to teach the women, girls and children of the village to stand up for themselves. In truth, they were my teachers.

Sitting on these friendly rocks of the canyon there is nothing to do but shout out my gratitude and my love to the thrum of this world and to all the beings below who gave me a reason to stretch and grow myself. A positive difference was made. May my story inspire others to find their heart's own great courage and jump.

# Part One

JUMPING

# Jump!

Glancing to the left I can see the needle on the altimeter hovering around 6,000. Quickly my wide eyes return to the other side, to the open door of a tiny plane roaring its way up into the skies over Molalla, Oregon. I gulp envisioning how very small those little houses below will be when we are 7,000 feet higher. Fear prickles my skin beneath the suit into which I am laced. My breath freezes in my chest and I start mindlessly, wildly praying to everyone, anyone, "Help!"

I am waiting for one word from the young instructor behind me; we will jump tandem. First will be the free-fall and then I will yank the cord for the parachute to open.

I have always believed that if I were in a plane on fire you would have to push me to get me out. I've never forgotten the scene in the Goldfinger movie when the bad guy is sucked out the plane's open window. I still side-step hatch doors on planes imagining they might somehow suddenly open and send me into the void. But, here I am about to jump out of a plane. Why? Because in 1992 I'm the eager student of an intense teacher. These are the early years of my self-discovery work. This is a Risking Workshop and my teacher, Ira, began by carefully asking each of his ten students to name the thing they were most afraid to do. I quickly, impulsively blurted out, "Jump from a plane."

It wasn't strategic, it wasn't wise, but it was true. The next thing I knew I was 50 miles from home at a flying school signing page after page of releases. They wanted to make sure I knew all the horrible things that might happen for which they were not in any way responsible — engine failure, parachute failure, tangles in telephone lines and paralysis. I am numb by the time we climb into the plane. All the way up a screech of fear is escalating within me when I hear the word:

"JUMP!"

I do. I jump and to my joy, to my absolute amazement, it is clear I'm not falling but instead floating like an autumn leaf on a playful breeze. My only problem is that I can't stop smiling and the wind hurts my open mouth. I can't stop. I float and smile my way all the way down. When I hit the ground and untangle myself from the parachute I run for my journal wanting to write a reminder to myself for ever after, "Always head into the fear, so much life waits there."

That jump from the airplane was perhaps my most literal dramatic jumping experience but the figurative one from Portland, Oregon to the Limpopo Province of South Africa in 2002 was way up on the chart. A graph of my sixty-two years would reveal a pattern of leaping between continents and across countries. In the middle of the night it can occur to me that this pattern hints at escapist, impulsive tendencies, but in the light of day I prefer to think I was born with a great sense of possibility and a healthy addiction to growth. When I consider my father at 95 years———blind and nearly deaf and taking his weekly recorder lessons———I know that this imperative to keep moving forward is in my world both by nature and by nurture.

In retrospect I understand exactly why any one of my many leaps was necessary at a particular point in time. How my job or my marriage or my longing to learn made the status quo too small, the walls too solid. At those moments it always seems vital to find my courage and take a leap rather than opt for certain but lifeless security. I have a ruthless streak when it comes to living my life. Inevitably I discard whatever appears to be in my way and stretch towards that which sounds the more perfect note.

After a year of treatment for breast cancer there was no choice other than to make a grand leap. It was time to leave the rarified Portland community where I was cozied up with family and friends, clients and students. After spending most of the '90s in trainings and workshops, sitting in processing circles or on meditation cushions, teaching or being taught, I knew deep in my bones it was time to get up and get out there. It seemed all that I had been learning and doing was preparation and it was now time to see what I could do. I was hungry. I wanted to gorge on hope and beauty, kindness and delight. I was ready to leap and Africa crooked her finger beckoning me.

"Jump," she whispered, "Jump."

And I did.

## First of Many Sundowners with Vicky

The late afternoon sun pours in the window as I lie on the bed in my circular hut, rondavel. I stare at the peak of the thatched roof and wonder if I really will find something outside this little nest, tucked in the confines of the botanical reserve. I think of this new world of mine as a set of Russian nesting dolls. This rondavel, my bedroom, closet and bath would be the very smallest doll. Next up would be the container of the Botanical reserve with its big, old, river-fed trees, the roar of the Blyde River, and impala, zebra, and baboons wandering freely about up the dirt roads, through the bush, into our yard. The vast canyon itself is the next biggest doll. It holds the body of the reserve. I remember the time several years ago when a group of us naively set off on a 'guided' kayak adventure down the Blyde River from the top to the dam at the base. It was wondrously wild, and we were lucky to come away with only bruised knees and elbows. One could imagine a leopard poking his head round any of the many curves we negotiated.

I continue my game. If I am only allowed four Russian nesting dolls, which is how I remember the set, the biggest would be what for most of the last century was the South African province of the Transvaal, Dutch for 'above the Vaal river'. It is the land the Afrikaner trekkers settled during the 19th century, far from the British-dominated southeast. They saw this land as theirs to fence, to graze their stock, and to grow their crops. But it is also the land of the sweet grass favored by all the grazing bucks and their predators. This is why Paul Kruger placed his famous public game park within this northern corner of the Transvaal.

Kruger National Park, 7,500 square miles, an area nearly the size of New Jersey, is home to all the wonders of the African animal world. This park is where I first saw a regal, old bull elephant gliding across a grassy field. Here, it is the humans who are caged in camps for the night while the animals roam free. This Transvaal where it never freezes is paradise for the fruit tree farmers and the animals. On the potato shape of South Africa we are within the northern curve at the top. It would take me a day to drive north to Zimbabwe, or east to Mozambique, or west to Botswana, and five hours southwest to Johannesburg.

I shake my head from my daydreaming and let myself be drawn by the soft sounds of wind and crickets outside the door. I decide to head out, to walk down the dirt roads of the reserve and maybe have a chance to meet the woman who just bought the lodge at the center of the Botanical Reserve.

"So, how did you end up here?" she asks.

Sitting on the edge of the courtyard, or lapa, with the new owner, Vicki, I consider how honest I should be in my response to her simple question. The tailored, button-down shirt and skirt she wears look like the dress of someone who sits at a desk in an office, not on the edge of a stone porch, under a thatched roof, looking out at the craggy peaks of the Drakensberg Mountains. She has bought this lodge in the Blyde River Botanical Reserve, and her own answer to her question is clear. She is in South Africa to run a business. Her outfit is in marked contrast to my own worn shorts, careless tee shirt and sturdy Teva sandals. I can see the sharp intelligence in her blue eyes. Though her painted nails are longer than I can possibly imagine, she feels familiar to me. Some people don't ask questions and some ask questions without really wanting the answer, but she seems genuinely curious and I decide to give her the kind of bone honest answer I would give to my close women friends in Portland.

"I first came here on a tour with an enlightened woman, my spiritual teacher. It's her homeland and I fell head over heels in love with the country."

Could one really fall in love with a country? I consider how it sounds, and try to explain. "At least it felt the same as falling in love———wide open, happy, delighted by each small thing, each big thing." I laugh remembering, "I couldn't sleep with the excitement of it all, the wonder."

She smiles, "I know that feeling. I'm still in love with Kenya." Vicki grew up there, she tells me, just down the road from the famous lion, Elsa. I nod, having been a voracious reader of African literature for ages. I know Elsa. In a sense, Vicki is still at home, both in the British Commonwealth and also the African bush. I, by contrast, have come to an alien world with only a vague mission in mind.

"Visiting here on a trip with a teacher is a long way from moving here," she says. "And you have now moved here, is that right?"

"Yep, right."

There is quiet as we sit looking out over the grassy lawn where several young impalas chase each other, playing tag in the late afternoon's soft light.

After that trip, I tell her, I still lived and worked as a counselor and yoga teacher in Portland, but more and more, I worked with Leslie and her group to raise money and awareness for the AIDS orphans here. I flash on those days when my sense of belonging with that group of seekers was so complete. They saw this Blyde Canyon reserve on their second South African tour, and I couldn't jump in fast enough when they told me about it.

"I remembered these mountains from our trip."

I lift my eyes to indicate the range of red orange cliffs in front of us. Who could resist?

"To be a part owner of a plot here. Well, it was kind of like 'I had a farm in Africa. . .'"

She laughs, catching my reference to Isak Dinesen's *Out of Africa*.

I tell her that four of us trundled around in rain boots one wet day with the builder, the son of the couple who sold her the lodge. She nods somewhat grimly, and I guess there is probably a story there. The builder helped us find a wonderful old weeping boerbaum tree up on the high side, plot 56. I indicate the direction with my hands. So we bought the plot and had the home built beneath it. I tell her that she'll meet Ramani one of these days. She's a redhaired Texan who writes and then stages her one-woman shows. She flits in and out. And Leslie is here now.

"She was my teacher."

Vicki raises her eyebrow, catching my past tense. I tell her that we were just finishing the home here on the Reserve when this happened. I indicate my near-bald head and pause to consider how to explain how hard the bout with cancer and its wretched treatments pushed me. I do still wonder if I truly would have jumped so far, followed my heart so impetuously, without the caw of death on my shoulder.

Vicki runs her hand through her own blonde hair as though trying to feel my experience. The small gesture of empathy suddenly makes my eyes well up.

I go on. Chemo knocked me off my feet, showed me things about myself I'd never been forced to face before. A tear runs down my cheek. Quickly, I wipe it away with the back of my hand. In my weakened state I have few filters, tears come up often and spill over despite my surroundings. My defenses have disintegrated. I don't have an option, my tenderness is on display whether I like it or not.

I remember the awful day I woke with hair covering my pillow. It was the day I'd been dreading. Radiation threw me into menopause, but this next indignity felt even worse. My belly contracts with the memory of that loss. How can I explain how it felt to someone I hardly know? I re-envision my image in the mirror that day. I sat in front of the mirror with scissors in my hand, lifted the remaining hair and, what didn't fall out in my hand, I chopped off. When I had finished the job, I just stared at myself.

Her brow is creased, but she says nothing.

To see myself so bared, so down-and-out ugly, shocked me, humiliated me, even just sitting there all by myself. Tears roll down my face, but I'm past caring as the memory takes over. Vicki reaches out to touch my knee.

"I was broken somehow, a slave or a prisoner. And as a woman . . . that's where the shame burned, and I seemed to shrink." A small shudder passes through me. "I saw in my eyes the shame of a woman without a shred of dignity, powerless and alone."

Her next question takes the tone down. It is reasonable.

"Was it because you were accustomed to being good looking?"

I consider this.

"Yes, but that would have just made me angry. This was worse, somehow."

Just then a small furry head with saucer eyes and large ears peeks out of the V-neck of Vicki's blouse and we both laugh. The tension of my tale is broken. The bushbaby, a big-eared primate about the size of a squirrel, has been napping in her ample cleavage and is waking up as the light fades. She gently reaches in and draws out the small being, making soothing sounds.

She tells me that her family took in strays in Kenya. As she strokes the small body now curled on her chest, I get a glimpse of her wild child self, not too far beneath the tailored clothing. She told me earlier that after eighteen years running a successful business in Australia she impulsively threw it all over to buy this lodge and moved here to manage it. Her husband will follow. I would bet she had been way too well behaved for way too long in Australia.

She looks up and says sincerely, "Sorry. Go on, I am interested."

I can almost feel her problem-solving mind whirring away at what I've presented. After a bit, stroking the now restless young animal, she asks her next question with a logician's curiosity and precision. What do I do now that I have the new sense of "degraded woman?" What does that lead to?

I shrug. It still seems a puzzle to me.

"I'm still gnawing on it," I say.

What I see for the first time is a part of myself that had been very well hidden. A sense of insecurity haunts me, and I don't know how this new self-knowledge fits into my future here. I have no idea what I will actually do here. How can I have moved across continents and not know what I'm going to do?

"All I know is what it won't be. It won't be like anything from the past," I say.

That means no counseling or teaching, or working with a spiritual teacher or focusing on AIDS orphans. Something new will appear, I'm hoping. I want to make a difference in the world somehow and right now. I don't know how it will look, but that is why I'm here.

An image flashes into my head but it's too out-there to share. It's a picture I once saw of the biblical Judith, raising her sword to slay the enemy general, Holofernes, leading her people to victory. I can't say that to Vicki but I tuck it away. "Tyrant slayer." I like the sound of it.

She nods, reflectively.

The sun is beginning to turn the cliffs a rich, deep orange, a signal that I need to walk back up the dirt road to my home before the night takes over. We stand, and I feel an awkward shyness, exposed after sharing these intimacies in our first real meeting. But she seems to have taken it in stride. She isn't backing away. Maybe she will be a friend in this new world of mine.

Walking with me to the road, she cautions, "Watch out for the baboons. They aren't scared of women."

I shake my head at that with a grimace and we both have to laugh at the irony. I take my leave, musing on our conversation.

Walking carefully down the road I avoid the deep crevices created by the heavy spring rains, and wonder if it was vanity, as Vicki suggested, having my good looks taken from me. But no, I argue with myself, it just isn't enough to explain the intensity. I scan my past for something deep enough to fill those eyes I saw in the mirror with such shame. Yes, my father found me willful and selfish, and came after me with a sharp tongue. My husband couldn't be faithful and left me in his own grand quest for freedom. But neither matches that ancient, almost primal pain I saw that day in my eyes.

I freeze hearing a rustle in the bush and try to peer into the dense tangle of trees, vines and brush. Nothing moves. I go on, stop to listen. Again I hear a creak of wood in the bush and I yell out. It feels great. I try a growl. That feels better, and so I growl my way all the way home, unchallenged.

## A Weaving Coop in Trouble?

Each day I can feel more creativity bubbling up within, but I have no way to play beyond caring for my increasingly less fragile self. It's a delight to feel the bubbling after too long in the weird chemo land of not-life. Still, there are moments when shadows of doubt creep into my thoughts, darkening the landscape and prickling my chest with fear. Will I find something to do, someone to help, a really juicy reason to be here?

I register movement just at the edge of my vision as so often happens in this bushveld neighborhood. Sometimes it is the small movement of a butterfly, a bird or the larger disturbance of a troop of curious baboons. But today it's a bushbuck, a doe, come to graze on the new grasses outside my open window. She is spooked by some movement and stands frozen with only her large brown eyes darting from side to side. Slowing, deepening my breath, I get very still, trying to soothe her and lure her into trusting enough to begin daintily clipping the grass once again. Maybe she will even allow her baby to come out of hiding. I watch as her vigilance dissipates and she lets her head sink back down to the grass.

Seeing my head's bare silhouette reflected in the glass of the window reminds me of those aged stone busts of Egyptian goddesses. It was always that peculiarly vulnerable curve of their back skull which touched me. Maybe I dropped my long hair like the multitude of mayfly wings I sweep from my small patio after rainstorms. The mayflies and me, beginning this phase, newly molted but please, please not emptiness and aloneness and too many books or horrors, the temptation of sucking on cigarettes when there is nothing else to feed me.

The rest of the buck family has appeared. The male with close, proud horns cresting his bent head is watchful and the new spring baby is all spindly legs and eyes and ears too big for the fragile frame whose every rib I can trace and every breath I see going in, going out. This family scene brings to mind my aged parents in their cozy home half a world from here. My connection to the Portland world runs through the thinnest of persnickety Internet lines. I feel a twinge of loneliness.

Please don't let this be a mistake, a flatfooted flop of a leap.

One hot day I happen upon a new crafts co-op in the small farm town of Hoedspruit where we do our banking and shopping. Stepping through the front door I see on the walls some garish acrylic paintings, which the heavy woman sitting at the counter proudly claims are her own. She's busy with a book that looks like an accounting ledger. She casually waves me back to look around.

Overstuffed cloth angels with plaid bows, crosses decorated with flowers and pithy sayings fill the front shelves. I now recognize this is the type of work crafted by the local Afrikaans women. They don't appeal to me, but I see some weavings in the back corner that look different, more like my idea of craft.

At the shelf where the three tapestries rest I finger the impeccable fringe and am intrigued. Who wove these tapestries with such precision? She———it must be a she———is using the same tapestry weave that I used years back on my own hand-built, wood-framed tapestry loom. I remember those long lovely mornings when I would sit cross-legged before the loom working with my wool and my musings. I think there is a special species of fiber-fabric lovers.

We daydream of worlds filled with mounds of gossamer silks, rough linens and bright, beribboned, hand-woven hammocks.

These tapestries are well woven, though the designs remind me of the '80s when weavings were popular as wall hangings. One has neat letters spelling out Happy Birthday with children holding hands; another is a Bible scene. The last one features a woman, a baby, and a round, thatched hut. They are old-fashioned designs but they touch me and I'm curious. Walking back to the front counter with one of the weavings in my hand, I ask the woman at the counter where they came from.

She tells me about a women's weaving cooperative out in Acornhoek. A woman named Shirley saw two of the women sitting on the side of the road with their weavings and felt sorry for them. She paid the fee to put their work in this store.

My interest mounts. Acornhoek is the black township 20 miles south of the reserve. It's where most of the maids and cooks and gardeners live. I've often passed the turnoff for Acornhoek, but I have never taken it.

The shop owner tells me that the weavers are in a bad way, quite desperate. She pulls a loose bit of paper from her pile and writes out Shirley's phone number for me.

"If you are a textile designer, maybe you can help them."

My degree in textile design from years ago doesn't quite qualify me as a textile designer in my eyes, but, maybe I can help, I think as I leave the quirky little store. I feel a wave of enthusiasm rising as I head back to the reserve.


## Meeting the Weavers

Shirley has set up a meeting for me with the weavers out in Acornhoek at 11. I'm ready to go, but it's still way too early. Opening the door, I step out and enjoy the clarity of the air after last night's wild spring thunderstorm. Throughout the night flashes of lightening lit my round room, rain lashed the thatched roof and winds knocked branches about. Thunder rumbled through my dreams, but now the world is washed and radiant, all hands clapping for the end of the long dry season.

Able, the not-really-a-gardener gardener, is raking leaves in the yard, so I pop over to announce that I'm heading for Acornhoek. He takes a break and rests his long frame on the rake, "You'll like it out there," he says with a lazy smile. "The folks are friendly and there are no bosses around."

It takes half an hour to get to the turnoff for Acornhoek, where it's immediately clear that I'm entering a different world. The virtual explosion of people, activity, sounds and happenings overwhelms me. The air smells of roasting meat, and loud dancing music blares from speakers outside one of the stores. Someone preaches into a microphone in front of another store. Families of goats cross the road in bursts of speed. The open market on my left is a jumble of stalls, vegetables and fruits in pyramids on the ground. Most of the traffic is on foot. Slowly the activity begins to thin and it seems I'm out of town. I drive past soft fields, not planted but not bush either, for all the trees have been chopped down. Small concrete homes with tin roofs and well-raked yards dot the fields along the road. There's not another car in sight. People are walking singly or in pairs on the side of the road, and are cutting off through the fields.

Soon, I see the weathered sign for 'Dingleydale' where Shirley's instructions say to turn right. It's a dirt road with deep potholes to negotiate. A swarm of little boys stands around a particularly deep rut with sticks in their small hands. One of the boldest waves at me, and the others smile, laugh and point at my car. Obviously, it's not a normal sight for them to see a white woman driving down their rutted road.

Seeing the peak of a church steeple, I turn into the drive of the Acornhoek Catholic Mission. Along the left side of the humble churchyard stands a long line of women and children. They carry empty plastic buckets on their heads and in their hands, so they must be waiting for water. Most are women with children by their side or tied on their backs. They have simple cloth bandanas covering their heads and lengths of patterned fabric hitched and tied at one shoulder, covering their skirts and shirts. I remember Able's comment and see that this is a world where white doesn't rule. It doesn't even exist.

I park under a tree and pause a moment to gather myself before going to knock on the door of what I assume is the studio across from the church. Shirley told me that this was the first Catholic mission in Acornhoek and it was the missionaries who had the idea to start a weaving cooperative back in the 70's. Then, ten years ago they stopped helping for some reason.

As I walk towards the weathered rectangular building one of the children playing in the grass sees me and runs to her mother, crying with fear of a white-faced interloper. Returning my attention to the building I see old foam rubber carefully stuffed in a broken window. The paint is chipping, with dark stains creeping up from the wet ground. Timidly I knock twice on the wooden slat door.

It swings open immediately and the friendly face of an older black woman smiles at me. She introduces herself in English, "I am Gertrude" and looks me straight in the eye with curiosity. I note the black pinafore reaching mid-calf that covers her dress, her kind brown eyes, missing teeth and earth-tempered hands. She shakes my hand, lightly touching her left hand to her right wrist. It signals something like respect, I think, though it feels strange, as she is older. She leads me into a big, high-ceilinged room. It echoes with emptiness, and my eyes fix on the small, silent circle of women seated in the center of the room. They seem to be waiting, waiting for me.

Gertrude introduces me to each woman and I shake hands. Though the names pass by me completely I am busy taking in each of the six women. Regina is one name I catch, a woman dressed all in black from her headscarf to her dress, short cape and shoes. I'm drawn to her both because somehow I understand she is the leader of the group and because there is an unmistakable level of deep upset in her whole demeanor. As our hands touch our eyes meet and though she only holds my gaze for a few seconds before lowering her focus, I recognize the anguish and the anger. I wonder about the black she wears. Who died? I nod my head and gently squeeze her hand.

All the women are older than I am so they must have been born around the same time the apartheid system of separation between blacks and whites became formalized. Acornhoek was one of the homelands, Vicki told me, but these women look as though their roots were here before all the displacements and troubles began. They seem modest, humble, shy yet strong. It is no wonder they chose the extroverted Gertrude as their greeter.

I feel somewhat overwhelmed, slightly dizzy when I've completed the circle. Uncharacteristically, I find nothing to say. I'm not sure who speaks English and who doesn't, or how to break the silence, what to do to connect with these silent women. Gertrude asks if I would like to see the storeroom. I nod and allow her to lead me around the large space of the studio. I compare it to my own studio in Boston, which was 800 square feet, and figure it is half again as big. The ceilings are high, and on three of the walls there are big wooden frame looms. They're the same simple structure of the looms used by the Navajo weavers in the Four Corners of the southwest from the 1850s to the present. The standing looms, with the capacity to unroll the warp and roll up the weaving, are just like the looms of 16th century Brussels or the even earlier tapestry looms of Pakistan which produce the weft-faced kilim rugs. There is an ageless quality to these simple tools of the weaving trade. I notice the area where the spinning wheels stand, pedaled by foot, of course, and the hand-combs with teeth to straighten the rough wool, the spools to measure out the warp threads. This is a well-equipped spinning and weaving workshop that could be anywhere in the world, anytime within the last 150 years. The wooden looms were constructed by Father Graf, Gertrude says, a German.

Gertrude points to the supplies on the storeroom shelves, rusted tins of dye powder, rolls of brown paper that I assume are designs for their Bible scene tapestry. I browse about on the shelves and find several woven tapestries resting in a pile, one with a family around a fire. There is potential there, I know it. They have all the necessary tools, the equipment and the skill, but they need direction. Could I help them? I wonder.

"Builder's break," Gertrude says it again and then again until finally, I get it. They are taking the month long Christmas holiday break as all builders do throughout the country. It is the midsummer holiday from school and all building stops. It's curious; they must see themselves as some sort of builder, crafters. Today, the women came from their homes to the studio only to meet me. This partly explains the disused, lifeless feel of the studio, but not completely. I awkwardly ask if they would like my help.

" ...maybe I could help you?

Gertrude looks to Regina who nods and turns to the others, speaks in her language, Tsonga I think, and they nod. Gertrude quickly informs me, "Yes. We need help."

We are busy at home now," she mimics hoeing a field. "Planting our mealies, but we will be back to work here in the studio on January 13."

"Okay, I will be here on the 13th, too. Okay?" Again, I don't know how many understand my declaration but I prepare to leave for now, suddenly aware that they probably would rather be at home working in their gardens. I consider buying something, but decide against it.

I wave good-bye to the women and tell them, "I'll come on the 13th. Happy Christmas, Happy New Year."

They aren't too animated in response. It's as if they want to be polite but don't seem to believe me when I say I'll return.

Regina says, " We thank you so much for coming."

All five of them nod politely as Gertrude walks me to the door.

She has a twinkle in her eye and I can sense that she, for one, does believe I'll return to help them. She's an optimist. I am, too. Shaking her hand we both nod our heads. I will be back.

Driving through the newly greened bush I am soaring like the wide-open sky, filled with love for the raw, vibrant beauty around me and excited, very excited about this Mapusha Weaving women's co-op. I liked the women instinctively and I'm hoping, wishing, dreaming that maybe this signals the end of my own long dry season.

## The Word of Paul

I think about life sometimes as a dialogue between hopes and fears. When I'm hopeful, I manage to banish the fears. Yet deep down I know they're there, hiding, waiting for a chance to raise their voice and assert themselves. In the worst of cases, they're dressed as un-assailable logic. There are also times when fear and dread run the show, and hope is hidden. In these times, the challenge is to try to bring all that hope up to the surface and convince myself it is more than the wish-filled illusion of an idealist.

It's a dance that goes back and forth, and in this African world where there are so many chances to be startled, surprised or horrified in the course of a day, the dance between hope and despair can move quickly.

As I return from my first visit to Mapusha, I am brimming with hope, and even have the audacity to dream of making the cooperative bigger. It is the time of day when the setting sun hits the red cliffs of the Drakensberg so they shine as though the light comes from within them. I am walking down from my lonely house on the reserve to have my sundowner glass of wine with Vicki at the lodge and feeling full and excited with the potential of this cooperative I've found. Vicki waves from the circle of wicker chairs where we usually sit but she has someone sitting with her. As I round the lapa, I recognize that it's Paul, another plot owner at the reserve whom I have met before. He wears his graying hair in a scraggly ponytail. He is small and slight and never without his threadbare bush shorts. He claims to have learned his ways as a wildlife expert from the bushmen of the Kalahari and is filled with stories and opinions. It is never boring to sit with him, though never simple, but I'm perky this evening.

Vicki calls out and I sit down to join them. Mala the impala, Vicki's latest orphan, is nosing her arm impatiently. She wants her evening bottle of warm water and Paul is scoffing at this practice. Vicky just laughs him off and continues picking ticks off her charge as they wait for the bottle.

Paul turns his bright, hard eyes to me and asks, "And what have you been up to, Yankee?"

I let his somewhat nasty tone roll off and launch into the story of the weaver's co-op. He listens with his head cocked and then leans forward.

"Why don't you stay home and help the Native Americans?"

I am caught up short, stopped as surely as if the road suddenly ended in a wall of cement. I shake my head and my puzzlement sets him off on a tirade about foreigners and their misguided notions of help. He tells the story of the Dutch woman who tried to teach the people of a rural village how to use condoms by demonstrating on a broom handle. When she returned all the broom handles in the village wore condoms.

I have that confused feeling that makes my head feel cloudy and I'm not sure how to answer. I begin to talk about the women. He isn't impressed. He leans forward and I smell his bushy smell. His bone earrings dangle.

"What you don't understand is that the ones who are going to make it will make it without your help. The fittest aren't in your village anymore, they have escaped and you are about to begin work with the losers."

Vicki tries to smooth things over, to laugh a bit at Paul and his misplaced ferocity. But I have taken a hit. My bubble has been popped, it feels like a Bambi meets Godzilla encounter. He brushed aside my earnestness as so much foolishness, spoke disdainfully from the perch of wise South African to idiot Yank.

I go over his words in my head as I walk home following my flashlight's beam over the rocky dirt road. I don't believe him, won't let myself believe him, but I am hurt by the animosity with which he went after me. I didn't know that being an American do-gooder in South Africa could bring such a response. And, though I don't have enough respect for him to be totally crushed, he has kindled the voice of fear.

As I make myself a salad, I try to put it out of my head. I reach for my book but that slightly sick feeling stays in my stomach. Even as I let my mind loose into the world of the novel, my body remembers Paul's verbal blows.

It is past my usual sleep time, but I am watching the gecko on the wall poised above an unsuspecting moth. I rehash Paul's points and do what I can to strip them of validity. Remembering his other diatribes, I can take his words down at least an octave. He's hyperbolic, after all. He's a storyteller and a stirrer of note but he isn't exactly a bullshitter. I can subtract my sensitivity to being verbally attacked by a smart and angry man and his subtle preening as "the expert." But, I know that despite his English accent, he has been here for all of his 40 some years and he is much more of an expert on everything African than I am.

Is it true that I am being naive? Of course, naiveté is part of who I am and that won't change. If it were easy to help these rural women find themselves as artists and entrepreneurs, this corner of South Africa would be crawling with investors. I realize it's a long shot and bank on the hope that together we can defy the odds.

But is it true that I am about to begin working with the losers? Maybe these are the ones that lack the initiative to get out, get saved from the cycle of poverty. But maybe they have never had an opportunity. Who knows when the timing is such that one drop will overflow the cup and change the pattern? It isn't different, I tell myself, from working with clients in Portland, believing in them, and supporting the potential that lies just beneath the surface.

I wish I were at my good friends' comfy farm in Nelspruit, about two hours south. I met David and Neil when I was on a preliminary visit to help orphans. They encouraged and supported me endlessly. They gave me a hearty dose of their dynamic fighting spirit throughout the cancer diagnosis and radiation treatment. David was diagnosed with AIDS in 1984 on his 22nd birthday. Twenty years later, he is still going strong. I would like to see Paul try to face him down.

I kick off my wrinkled sheet and cross my arms behind my head. The gecko is creeping closer to the moth, which rests with wide-open wings on the frame of a picture. I switch off the light hoping to find peace in sleep, hoping the moth moves before the gecko swoops down.

## First Day on the Job

Driving into the mission yard I see a small child sitting on the front steps of the studio. She watches as I get out of the car and head in her direction. When it becomes clear that I am going to come right up to the steps where she is sitting, her eyes widen but stay fastened on me.

"Hello," I say with a smile.

This is too much for her. She has reached the end of her three-year-old courage and scrambles back to safety inside the studio. I stick my head in the open door and the women are all there. They are busy with tasks that spinners and weavers have been doing for eons. A couple of them card raw wool with bristled wooden paddles. One pedals an old wooden spinning wheel with a steady, whirring rhythm. The diapered child has curled up against Regina who is weaving on an upright floor loom.

I step inside and give a shy, generalized wave to the group, receive discreet nods in return. They continue with their work and so I walk towards the loom where Regina sits.

"Hello Regina, how are you?"

She turns towards me with restrained warmth.

"I am fine," she says as she places her hand on the small shaved head by her side. "This is Sampiwe, my granddaughter."

I squat down to Sampiwe's level and she turns her head towards me, slightly, but I don't risk speaking again, just smile. It takes a little while for her to retreat back into the quiet comfort of her granny's skirt.

I straighten to speak with Regina but pause, stymied by the vastness of my ignorance in this world. I don't know the rules of etiquette. I don't know what they need or want or how exactly I can help. But I know I like the way it feels here in the studio. She has turned her attention back to her weaving again. Her long, lean fingers move the wool into the space between the white warp threads and then beat it down with a crude wooden comb. She is comfortable with silence.

I ask her what she's making, for the small square of dark woven wool with the bright orange geometric doesn't look the right size for a tapestry.

"We have an order for 30 table mats from the Safari Lodge."

I nod and try to imagine these small squares on a table.

She chuckles softly, "It isn't much money, but it is money."

"And you have to card the wool before you spin it, dye it before you weave it?"

She nods.

"That is a lot of work."

I continue watching her fingers. I want to believe that if I am quiet enough, I can learn more about this woman, as if by osmosis. She is still wearing all black, but the grief and the anger I saw at our first meeting have receded.

Gertrude comes in the studio and walks directly over to shake hands and welcome me. She is late because of a sick grandchild at home. She tells me they need wool and she might know where we can get some.

For the next couple of hours I sit on a bench in the corner, quietly taking it all in, the grounded pace of the women as they ply this ancient craft I've always loved. Someone is singing softly and though I don't understand the words, I know it's a hymn. There are three Anna's in the studio, a tall very thin spinner Anna, a medium weaver Anna and a small spinner Anna. It doesn't seem any of these three speak English. They must have chosen the name Anna as their Catholic name, not the name given them at birth. Lindy is the weaver who did not attend my first meeting with the weavers. She is small, round and very shy though I instantly understand how much she knows about the craft.

No one suggests what I can do to help, but they seem unruffled by my presence. Sampiwe has come over to observe me more closely and I make a goofy face, entertaining her, teasing out a small laugh when suddenly the quiet rhythm of the room is broken as the wooden front door bangs open. A young woman with dreadlocks and tight jeans enters and surveys the room. By Sampiwe's smile I gather this must be her mother, Regina's daughter. She walks towards me and I'm aware of being examined carefully. I can almost taste her wary curiosity, wondering who is this woman and what is she doing here?

"I am Emerencia," she announces in confident English.

I introduce myself.

"You are from America?"

I nod. Everyone knows where I am from the moment I speak one word.

"Then why are you here?"

It is a strange and interesting question for me but I understand somehow that this young woman is bursting with her own ambition. This village must feel very small and constraining to her.

"I love this country more than I love America right now. It is more beautiful to me, more alive, more fun."

She nods reflectively, trying to take in my words.

I ask her if she has always lived here, near the mission.

"Yes," she says with a sigh.

She tells me that for a short time she left for Johannesburg and had a job at the airport, but then got pregnant. We both concentrate our attention on Sampiwe who is practicing making her small face into strange contortions. Emerencia tells me she returned to her mother's house three years ago. She raises her eyebrows and I get it. She's bored and restless in this rural world.

She tells me funny stories about Sampiwe, her struggle for power with her mother, her devotion to her grandmother. She sits on the table chatting with me, telling me about the women of Mapusha whom she has known her whole life. She was one of those babies who came on her mother's back and stayed as a part of the cooperative until she went to grade school. She is twenty-five, though I can't help but think of her as a girl. She is feisty and smart and I quickly sense that she will talk to me with a freedom that the older women never will.

She pulls her cell phone from her jean pocket to check and see if she has any messages.

"Do you know Alaska?"

I nod, puzzled.

"My sister used to live there," I tell her. "But I never went. It's very cold, and in the winter it's dark almost all day. Why do you ask?"

"I am thinking of going to Alaska to work on a fishing boat."

She makes this startling statement with the same brazen attitude with which she opened the door. But after speaking, she looks at me sideways, giving me a glimpse of what lies beneath the bravado.

"That's brave," I tell her, trying to picture this young South African woman working on a fishing boat in the arctic. "Do you know how to swim?"

"I can learn," she says with pride and reaches out her hand to Sampiwe, signaling it is time for them to go. She tells me she'll show me the Alaska advertisement tomorrow.

As they walk towards Regina, I realize this curious young woman hasn't asked me anything about myself other than why am I here. It seems as though she would be itching to know who I am and what am doing in this studio. If she doesn't ask, who will have the nerve to ask me questions?

## Buying Wool from a Skellum

My first task, as Gertrude suggested, is to find the co-op some wool. I search the phone book, call information and finally find the phone number of the now defunct Masana Weaving in Bushbuckridge. After many attempts I get through to a man named Henry, the manager, who agrees to meet me at the factory on Sunday. I am hesitant to go alone and a bit suspicious about having to meet on Sunday, so I ask Gertrude to come with me. She says that I can pick her up after church.

I get to the mission yard just as the church service finishes and stand watching the worshippers smile as they follow the choir onto the lawn. The choir is robustly singing a Christian hymn with an African cadence as they spill out the doors. I begin shaking hands with one after another of the church women. Sampiwe proudly wears a long white lace dress and follows me with her eyes, as I stand with her beloved gogo (grandmother). Gertrude wears a special Sunday hat and a well-pressed shirtwaist dress, ready to go. Her feet, usually bare in the studio, are fitted into shiny black pumps with a low heel. I usher her into the front seat of my car and we set off together for Bushbuckridge.

She tells me about her eight children; Prince, Foster, Susan, Wonder, Cecil, Peddy, Terry and Patty. One of her daughters died recently, which explains her black smock. She left behind a baby who isn't well, Sinthe. Despite the sad story, Gertrude seems to be enjoying our little journey and I feel free to ask her some of my questions. She both answers and laughs easily.

I have never been in the townships on a Sunday and I enjoy seeing all the Sunday outfits of the churchgoers walking along the side of the road. She explains that those wearing bright white robes with the deep blue trim are the Zionists. Regina, Gertrude and Lindy all attended the new Catholic mission school when they were young. She knows the year she was born, 1943, and she knows she was thirteen when s`he first came to the mission school. All of the students at the new school were required to become Catholics and choose a new name. That was the price of admission to the school, which provided books and uniforms at no cost. I try to picture her as a young girl walking into the little, dilapidated building by the studio, which was the one-room schoolhouse they attended.

Summing up her relationship to the weaving studio and the mission she says simply, "It is my home.".

Gertrude paints a picture for me of the most prosperous days of the co-op when there were 26 women working, many of them bringing their small children on their backs. They wove Bible-scene tapestries that the German Fathers helped them to sell at the Catholic churches throughout Germany. But now things are hard. The Fathers aren't German anymore, and the new ones from Spain want to build churches rather than participate in self-help programs. The women of Mapusha have been on their own for 10 years.

We drive through the quiet Sunday town of Bushbuckridge and turn down a side road and then another before we get to a chain-link fence with an empty guard hut. The crooked sign reads *Masana*.

Gertrude tells me to toot, and when I look puzzled she presses her hand on an imaginary horn and says "toot, toot" and then cracks up at her own joke. My tooting eventually rouses a man who looks the worse for wear———a big Saturday night at the local shebeen I would guess. Gertrude prevails with a stream of words in Tsonga and he opens the gate for us to enter.

We wait in the car, parked in the lot of this empty factory, and my skin crawls a bit despite my sturdy guide. I haven't seen another white face in the last hour and our surroundings look somehow threatening. Gertrude sits quietly with her hands folded in her lap and a faraway look in her eye. She is obviously practiced at waiting. I am not. Soon I'm tapping my feet and trying to call Henry on my cell.

If this weaving operation has really gone under, perhaps he will authorize a cheap sale of wool to its sister-weavery, Mapusha. This was the tack I was planning to take, a well-reasoned and elegant form of begging. I'll have to pay for the wool myself, as Gertrude had told me that they have earned no salary for several months. When something is sold they give the money to those who need it most  .

Henry arrives on foot wearing shiny shoes, slacks, and a belt beneath his belly. He proudly shows us into the showroom where samples of woven carpets are tumbled about. Gertrude bends to finger the carpet and gives me a raised eyebrow. She isn't impressed. We walk through the weaving factory looking at loom after loom. It's empty now but it is as though the ghost weavers had just yesterday stood up. They left their small colored butterflies of wool hanging from the half-finished geometric weavings on the looms, baskets of wool at their side.

Henry leads us into the wool storage room and tells us we can take what we need for R30 ($3.00) a kilo. It feels like a good deal to me, but Gertrude argues with him. I can't understand their words but the price goes down and Gertrude gets busy rifling through the bins to extract the spun wool she finds acceptable. Henry takes us to his empty office and carefully writes out a receipt for R200 when I hand him the cash. He calls his guard to help us get the big bags into the car. The guard asks if I have a cigarette. I don't, but I do have a five rand coin which he happily accepts as he squishes the awkward bundle into my trunk. I drive out the gate thrilled, but Gertrude harrumphs,"The spun wool is too thick, lazy spinning," she says, "Mapusha's wool is better and he, Henry, he is a skellum."

I'm not sure what that word means though I catch the drift, but for me the victory is bigger than the problematic source. We have wool. We can begin.

## A Cauldron, a Fire and Dyed Wool Galore

Leslie, my housemate and former teacher, has commissioned the weavers and spinners of Mapusha to make a runner for the hall of our home in the canyon, and today we will dye the wool for it, our first commissioned rug. I'm giddy with anticipation. I love color, all colors from the palest, sweetest pink to the most vivid, siren red and every shade in between. The alchemy of it fascinates me. I took courses on the chemistry of color back in the '80s at the Philadelphia College of Textile Science and Design and gobbled up books on color theory and the new field of color therapy. While I enjoy the science and the aesthetics, it is the magic of something white becoming something other that delights me. And, on this sunny day as I turn into Acornhoek to help dye the newly spun white wool, I have a bright sense that magic will prevail.

When I pull into my parking spot under the tree on the mission's lawn, I see Lindy, the shortest, quietest most competent of weavers, carrying a big tin tub on her head. I scramble out of the car and follow her to the "dying shed" which consists of a tin roof over a fire pit with long, heavy metal poles hooked and hanging horizontally from the beams. Gertrude is bent over, feeding the fire with twigs. Lindy deposits the washing tub on the ground and, without a word takes over the fire-tending as Gertrude picks up a long wooden pole with a hook taped to the end and starts off purposefully across the lawn towards the big old gnarly amarula tree. She lifts the hook high up into the branches and then pulls on one particular leafless branch. Sure enough, the branch comes crackling down through the others and she picks it up, puts it on her head and sets off for the next target.

One of the three Anna's has brought a bench out for me to sit on and there is a cardboard box full of jars and tins of dye. Sampiwe has joined us and together we peer with interest into the box. We have a game now. I say her name and she responds with mine, the sort of game required when you don't speak the same language. She has quickly cottoned to the fact that while African mamas and gogos take good care of you, they don't play with you the way this strange Judy does. She particularly likes to play tickle, for tickling means she gets to touch my white skin and she considers this a treat. Regina told me yesterday that during Sampiwe's morning bath in the plastic washtub she worked hard with a cloth trying to scrub her arm white, "like Judy's."

I stroke the soft skin of her lovely dark arm as Mapusha's big washing tub is filled with jugs of water collected from the borehole at the mission. All five women help with this task and I watch them walking towards the dye shed, strong and straight, with the full jugs on their heads.

Now, the heavy white skeins of newly spun wool drift in the clear water. Lindy pulls several out and with deft hands wrings away the excess water. She carries them to the big black iron pot on the fire where the water is bubbling. I have mixed orange, brown and red dye powders in a little rusted tin and Gertrude stirs the color into the roiling waters while Lindy carefully places one skein, then another, into the pot. Immediately, the white turns to a soft warm orangey pinkish brown that echoes for me the iron-filled earth of the canyon. Sampiwe and I watch as Gertrude draws one of the skeins out of the water with a stick to show me the color. I nod, pleased.

We watch the dyed skeins of wool being dropped in and pulled from the pot, wrung out again and hung over the metal poles. Lindy shows me how to put weight on the skeins to make the fibers straight, to pull the wet colored wool through my hands till it forms a smooth loop of fiber, and then hook it at the bottom and weight it with a stone.

We have created oranges and blues, browns, greens and grays in many shades, some lovely some less so. Lindy and Gertrude want me to be the color boss, and I do my best as they run the dyeing operation. It is sunny and warm as I look out over the village where the Mapusha women live. The Drakensberg mountains shimmer through the haze from our fire. Everything wiggles a bit in the smoke and I shake my head with the wonder of being here, dyeing wool over an open fire with Gertrude, Lindy and Sampiwe.

# Taking on the Boss of a Safari club

As I come to be a regular feature at the co-op, I begin to decipher the relationships and the ways of this group of six women who have come daily to the studio throughout the years, good times and bad. Regina is the chairperson. She and Gertrude have been best friends since they attended the newly opened Catholic mission, one-room school fifty years ago. In those days, Gertrude says, there were still elephants, lions and trees in the bush of their village, Rooiboklaagte.

Anna Mbetsi and Anna Mduli eat lunch with Gertrude and Regina. They share the rounds of cornmeal pap made in the morning and sit on the floor, legs long and backs straight, and then stretching out on grass mats with their aprons over their faces for a short nap before going back to their looms and spinning wheels. Anna Nduzulkula and Lindy eat on the other side of the room. I ask Lindy one day why she eats here, away from the others and she replies, "Because it is my place."

Serves me right for asking. The women are invariably polite as can be with me but I come to understand that mealtime is not social time. It is time for eating, which is a serious business where hunger is so real. They speak together only after they have eaten their mound of white pap with a side of whatever vegetable is in season, and after carefully washing their hands in the communal, enamel bowl that sits with a hand-cloth in the center of their circle.

I have learned to bring my book and sandwich and eat out on the front step. It feels better than bumbling about in their private realm. Plus, I get to watch the people waiting for water and usually interact in some fun way with their children.

I often stop on my way to the co-op and buy a bag of apples or a box of cookies. Offering the goods to the women is a ritual of giving and receiving. I offer the bag to Gertrude and she claps her hands together in thanks before receiving her gift. I go around the circle with my gifts and they thank me. Sometimes I am inspired to extend their eating repertoire with something like broccoli or roasted sunflower seeds. They delight in the new experience and decide that broccoli is good if one has plenty of mayonnaise to dip it in.

They all tend their gardens with great devotion. Regina tells me that their mothers fed their families almost entirely from the gardens. It is part of their rhythm; corn is planted when the rainy season starts in December and then beets and tomatoes, spinach and onions when it has cooled down a bit, ground nuts and yams in the summer. Their diet has little variety other than the seasons. So whatever I bring is a great treat for them.

The weavers have completed the order for 30 table-mats. I have been trying to call the lodge, to arrange for the mats to be collected. Finally, desperate to get the women their due, I set off with Gertrude to visit the lodge, give them the mats and collect the money. We drive down the road towards Kruger Park and, and I ask Gertrude if she has ever been there. She says that during Apartheid blacks weren't allowed in the park, and since then she hasn't had the money. I know she has a full household of children and grandchildren, 13 altogether.

We find the safari lodge, park, then wander around until finally a blonde woman with an Afrikaans accent asks if she can help us. I can feel both her curiosity and judgment of me with Gertrude at my side. Gertrude is behaving with dignity as she greets both the black maids and the white secretary. I explain the mats, the unanswered phone calls, and she phlegmatically calls back to the manager.

Jock comes out all smiles and greetings for me and for Gertrude. He apologizes for the phone problems. He will happily take the mats. But he is afraid that the safe is locked and the key off in Hoedspruit with his partner. I can feel my hackles starting to rise as I remember the women sitting in a circle carding the wool for these mats. As a bush guide, Jock has spent many hours pleasing foreigners, but he isn't pleasing me. Gertrude is quiet and polite and I, accordingly, restrain myself. But it bothers me that we won't be returning with the money for the women of Mapusha. I pointedly tell Jock I will be back tomorrow morning.

It is late and I offer to take Gertrude to her house. This is the first time I have been down into the village. We bump along the dirt road riddled with cracks, crevices and potholes from the recent heavy rains. She gestures to the left where a wire fence is gaily hung with numerous clean children's pants, shirts and skirts. There is one big house and then a whole row of shacks with crooked tin roofs held down with rocks. Mango trees with ripe fruit hanging and a big garden surround the house.

Children of various sizes come out of the house curious to see what is happening. Their names are a blur but I focus my attention on Sinthe, a two-year-old whose mother died at her birth. Her aunt has taken over caring for her, which must be a big job as the child neither walks, nor talks. She begins bouncing happily when she see her grandmother, making loud sounds of greeting which make everyone else in the yard laugh. An older man with thick glasses is suddenly before me.

He greets me enthusiastically. He is Ephram, Gertrude's husband, he says, and the first black man to make white sugar for the whites. He takes me on a tour of Gertrude's garden, which he says is his as well since he keeps the birds away while Gertrude is at Mapusha. As I leave, Ephram tells me to come visit them again. I will.

The next morning I decide to save time and go directly to the safari lodge to pick up the money owed the co-op. I know how much they need it. As I pull into the lodge a bakkie is pulling out and the blonde receptionist informs me that pick-up truck was the management going to town. She doesn't have a key to the safe. She informs me that they will be back in an hour. I put out my hand for the phone.

I am burning by the time Jock finishes his lame explanation of why the money isn't available. "Do you have any idea how much time went into these mats? Do you have any idea how many people are waiting for the measly R300 that you owe them?" I go on and on, my voice gaining volume as I accuse him of taking advantage of the women and treating them without respect. There is a long silence when I finally run out of steam.

"We will bring the money to the cooperative today," he says. I exit the office with a curt nod to the receptionist. It's the first time I have been called on to stand up for Mapusha, to raise my voice against the bad treatment they receive from people who look a lot like me.

I like it. Slayer of tyrants in action.

## Designer on the Job

I drive through eucalyptus tree farms on the way to Hazyview for a meeting with a woman who needs a living room rug and has heard of the weavers in Acornhoek. I am crossing my fingers and holding thumbs, as they say here, that she will place an order that would give the weavers a moneymaking project during my coming six-week absence. Next week I'll be returning to Portland for a visit, and for my Dad's 93rd birthday party. I have carefully explained to the women when I am leaving and when I will be back, but they look doubtful. Naturally, they understand that I need to celebrate my father's 93 years, but they wonder why I would return. What they don't grok is that the weaving studio and the women of Mapusha are the center of my everything at the moment. I sleep them, dream them, and wake with ideas and questions, worries and wonders and visions for them, day in and day out.

I dressed myself up for this appointment with orange sandals and big earrings. I tried to put myself in the right mode with an imaginary interior designer hat but it sits wobbly on my head. Yes, I did go to design school and worked with textiles but I was never an interior designer in my own American world. I am not sure how I will pull it off in this very different design world of white South Africa. I turn off the big road that I drive often between David and Neil's farm in Nelspruit and the Blyde reserve, clutching my directions and pushing my sunglasses up I manage to make the right turn and the left turn, and park in front of a well-gated, red brick house with the correct numbers. I sigh. These bricks signal a certain kind of linear aesthetic that is a far cry from my own preference for quirky, rock walls joined by old, leathered leadwood beams. But try I must, so I reach through the window to buzz the intercom and make my way into this fortress.

I am greeted first by a pack of dogs. A tall blonde woman hurries up behind them, yelling at them to stay. Since these dogs are part of the alarm system they aren't supposed to be friendly to strangers, but they seem to know I am both white and a woman. They mill about my legs as Alison comes up and shakes my hand. I watch her pick up one of the little ones. She has the usual mix of large intimidating dogs and little barker types. She has a certain primness that reminds me of cocktail parties that my parents had in our home in the Philadelphia suburbs in the early 1960's. I imagine her in a shirtwaist dress with bobby pins in her permed hair.

As we walk through her tiled entryway into the living room, I begin to tell her how I met the weavers. Then I see, just as I feared, that the living room is a huge rectangle space with barred windows and a big, black metal fireplace taking up at least a quarter of the room. The furniture consists of a couple of heavy wooden chairs with covered cushions tied on the chair backs.

We sit. Naturally, she asks if I would like tea or coffee and, as usual, I opt for the coffee though I know it will be Nescafe in a little bowl with a little spoon on a tray. Only the small dogs are allowed in the house, and they surround her chair. I scan the empty room with its concrete walls and cold tiles on the floor.

"I do think a woven rug would be lovely here in your living room," I say, and watch to see how she will respond. She picks up the sausage dog and nods a quick yes as she goes to fetch the tea tray.

I look at my orange sandals on the tile floor and know I haven't pulled quite the right string here for the interior designer look. I imagine she would expect nails and heels and if pants are involved, they should be tailored and pressed. Someone once described me as always in need of a safety pin. It was funny back in Boston days, post-college, but is less so as I sit in an uncomfortably hard chair in this empty room. I try to visualize a rug that would suit both the room and its owner. Free-flowing curves won't work. The rug will have to be geometric and most certainly symmetrical.

When she returns with my coffee I ask her about the plans for the room, the color scheme. As she starts to speak, suddenly, I get it. She is scared to make decisions on the design front and doesn't feel confident that she can make the house a perfect expression of her most perfect self. That makes it easier. I'll have to be the confident one, full of design ideas and big on decisions.

"I think you want to pick up the warm tones within the tiles, orange and rust, a little pink and a touch of yellow. Let's measure how big it should be and then we can work on the design."

We're off. I just take over and leave with a check for Mapusha for half the cost of the rug and a design idea that popped into my head just when I needed it. I'm sure the Mapusha women can dye and weave the rug I described to Alison, but I will have to leave with little more than a hope that the rug will be ready to deliver when I return in April.

## Rug Number One Completed

It is time to cut our first real rug, Leslie's rug, off the loom and I am busy with my camera taking pictures of Gertrude and Lindy with this piece they have spent the last month weaving. They have been weaving for over 30 years and yet this is the first one with me on the team. As they reached higher and higher their scaffolding had to be improvised until, at the top of the rug they maneuvered three of the big, wooden rectangular tables one on top of the other. They have tied their rickety wooden stepladder to the table pyramid and they climb up it each day to finish the 12-foot runner. Lindy says very few words but I know she isn't happy about being so far from the earth. Gertrude, on the other hand, is just one of those can do, will do, whatever must be done type of people. You can see it by the way she walks, straight and purposeful no matter if she is moving across the field, up the ladder, into the garden. It is she who has the scissors in hand to snip the cotton threads of the vertical warp and, as the final thread is cut, the rug slithers down to the floor. We applaud.

All the women gather round as the bottom of the warp is cut off of the thick wooden beam, which is the base of the loom. We lay the rug out on the floor. Despite its unfinished edges, it looks beautiful. It is an African landscape with hills and valleys, gentle curves in the colors of the land - grays, browns, yellows and deep rusty orange, dusty greens. I am excited, for this rug is an indication of what these weavers can do, and it looks sellable to me. It is meant for the hall of the main house at my home at Blyde but it doesn't feel quite right for that space to me. It is more like a painting that should hang on a wall.

If it must be on the floor, the surroundings would have to be starkly plain so as not to compete with the life in the weaving. This is the first time I have ever designed a rug for someone else to weave. They are more skillful weavers than I, and I am shocked by the power of the product. The women sit together on the smooth concrete floor of the studio and carefully knot the fringe of our first rug.

I wish Leslie were here to see it, and to celebrate this little milestone in my apprenticeship at the co-op. I will take it home and lay it on the waxed, tiled floor of the big house in the bush, but there is no one else to witness the moment. Gertrude and Lindy carefully sweep the rug of any fuzz, clip away stray ends and it is officially finished. They fold it up and put it into my arms. I smile my pleasure at this, our accomplishment.

I drive home knowing both that I worked with the women to create a beautiful piece of weaving and that the rug will not work in the hallway for which it was designed. I worry about this piece of the puzzle. It seems with my design and their skill we can create beautiful rugs but can we create the right rug for the designated spot.

My time in design school and in my Boston studio didn't prepare me to work as a professional interior designer. I loved the materials and the process of weaving and the creativity. I could get lost in each tapestry I wove, watching how each thin strand of wool changed the whole beneath it.

I gave one of my pieces to my yoga mentor entitled, "Flow." It was a small rectangle of tiny, tiny shiny threads woven in a random pattern of flowing colors. It looked lovely framed in her dressing room but it would be a whole different thing to design a rug for her dressing room. I wonder if I can morph my childlike enjoyment of the process into a professional slot. The stakes are high. With the Mapusha women so very close to the edge, it isn't just play anymore.

I take the rug to the lodge and proudly show it to Vicki and the guests and the staff and just about anyone passing by. We sit on the deck and watch the wildebeests and zebras grazing on the lawn. The rug lies spread out on the terrace and I enjoy watching the colors subtly change in the fast approaching dusk.

Vicki, ever the business woman, asks, "How many rugs this size would they have to do each month to keep the co-op going, pay for salaries and materials?"

I shrug, my eyes still on the rug.

"I think this should be called *African Landscape*." I am not willing to venture off this moment and really have no idea what the next move for the co-op should be business-wise, and Vicki knows this.

My attention goes back to the rug. I know something about it doesn't quite fit. The woven woolen pieces are really a craft of Germany not Africa, and wool is hardly the right material for the hot and dry climate of the lowveld. It is dusk and Vicki is still wearing her bathing suit with a sarong. It is hard to imagine a woolen rug in this scenario. But, again, I let this understanding slip to the background as I relax, sip my wine, and let myself rest in admiration of our rug for the moment.

The bushbaby sticks his head up out of Vicki's bathing suit bra. We laugh. My leap into the unknown with the vague notion of making a difference shows signs of working. I'm making a difference. I love having my feet on the ground, my attention on the very real world of the women of Mapusha, and even the problems seem exciting. There can be no better medicine to help me heal myself.

## Breakfast with Mom and Dad

Opening my eyes a blue wall fills my vision. A blue wall? I fully focus and remember. I'm home. I let myself sink down, relishing the familiar comfort of this slant-ceilinged room on the second floor of my parents' home. Its small confines have been what I've called home since selling my own Portland bungalow three years ago, freeing me for the world of service and adventure. I scan my favorite tchotchkes on the shelves, the delicate wooden carving of a deer, the Italian triptych of the Madonna that belonged to Ira's Communist aunt, the crudely hewn bust of a tur-baned African woman that I bought in Paris years ago. Glancing at the clock I calculate the nine-hour time gap and imagine what's happening in the studio now. They have finished lunch and are working at their looms again, weaving the rug for the Hazyview woman.

I close my eyes and murmur, "Let it be good."

Familiar breakfast sounds waft up the stairs from the kitchen along with the smell of the never-quite-strong-enough coffee brewing. Pulling a favorite ratty, red sweatshirt over my head I picture the six prunes in a small china bowl placed before Dad on the table. Brushing my teeth I consider how meals have always been like a metronome in their steady lives, marking time, meal by meal, day by day.

Walking down the stairs, I see Dad sitting at the table. His hear-ing is bad and his vision worse and he doesn't hear my arrival. I have a moment to see him without his public, relational face. He looks so gentle now and yet, that is not how I would describe the Dad of my youth. His bathrobe is cinched round his narrow waist and his hand is to his ear, delicately tinkering with the controls on his hearing aid. I know how much he wants to be able to hear everything at the table this morning. His other hand rests on the newspaper he can no longer read. I admire his cheery attitude despite the physical trials of being ninety-three.

"Everything OK in there?" He is speaking to Mom who's in the kitchen preparing their eggs and toast.

"Just fine. Did I hear Judy come down?"

"Yes you did, here I am." Walking into the dining room I touch Dad's hand and he lights up.

"How'd thee sleep, kiddo? What a treat to have thee here with us." These days his four children seem to bring him nothing but pleasure, and his enthusiasm for all of our projects and problems is boundless.

Mom comes in with a plate in each hand and I go to pour myself a mug of coffee before joining them at the table. It's not the same table as the one we grew up with but, any table where eating happens is a center in this world of my family.

"We go casual for breakfast now-a-days," Mom says with a gesture of apology to their bathrobes and slippers.

It must wear on her, increasingly, having to be the eyes, ears and hands for her partner of 57 years. I resolve to amuse them, and launch into a story about my contest with Sampiwe. We were competing to see who could walk furthest balancing a book on her head. The four-year-old won. Mom is delighted with my tale, giggling as she carefully carves loose the segments of Dad's half orange with a small curved knife.

She says that at Germantown Friends School, she and her classmates had to balance books on their heads to help with their posture. I try to imagine Mom in her Quaker school balancing a book on her head. She was shy then and shy dealing with me as a teenager as well. It was only my bout with cancer that broke through her inhibitions and a more lioness-like version of my mother finally emerged. She traveled alone to South Africa to support me between the lumpectomy and the start of radiation and as I watched her climb down the steps of the small aircraft she looked both so frail and so brave that my own long-held barriers softened. She fell for Africa as completely as I had, and keeps the small photo album of our time there by her bedside. We finally have something to share.

I entertain them for an hour with tales of my South African world and Mom declares she wants to order two Mapusha rugs. Dad offers to help me with a fundraising letter and I can see he is already working on the wording in his mind. As they disappear into their room to dress properly for the day, I remain at the table and muse on the simple fact that for the first time in my adult life I am doing something they can understand. Despite their earnest efforts, they never understood my years of emotional processing or spiritual seeking. What I'm doing now is the type of social action that is the basis of their religion.

Mom comes out wearing a pastel printed shirtwaist, her sensible, corrective shoes neatly tied and her short, white hair well brushed.

"I think one of the rugs should go right here in the front hall and one in the TV room." she announces. "And you will do the designs? Full price now, we don't want any family discounts." She is very pleased with this scheme of hers to help the women of Mapusha.

I go get the tape measure and am crawling around on the floor getting the measurements when Mom says quietly, "You know, I once dreamed of being a missionary in Africa." I'm startled and sit back on my heels with that peculiar sense that something important just happened.

"You did?"

She nods her head, a little self-conscious at this personal disclosure, and moves on, changing the subject to the more pedestrian schedule of the day, asking if I might be able to take the dog for a walk in the woods with Dad this afternoon.

"Your father would so enjoy an outing with you."

I agree to the walk at the traditional time, following the afternoon nap, but I'm still caught by Mom's strange admission. I have heard her say that she wanted to be a lawyer, which always seemed sadly strange to me for she really is no logician. But a missionary in Africa? I doubt anyone had ever heard this fantasy. The information makes everything go quiet as though there is something here that I don't quite fully understand, something I need to understand.

We have always been so very different. I was a girly girl who loved pretty clothes, thumped out romantic show tunes on the piano and dreamed of being a beautiful, brave heroine. In these lofty realms my practical mother had nothing to offer to me. One of our few epic battles came at the start of the school year and rested on shoes———saddle shoes or loafers. She was adamant that I wear saddle shoes on my first day at the public middle school and I was vehemently saying absolutely no. We were in the car, in the garage and I was hysterical at the outrage of it all. She couldn't possibly understand the importance of my appearance at a new school on the first day. Maybe it was fine for her to wear sensible shoes and dull clothes but my fury that day was over the larger issue, the unfairness of having a mother who didn't understand my world at all. I never did wear those saddle shoes to school. That's partly why it startled me today to have her tell me her youthful fantasy. One could call me a missionary of sorts.

I go over in my mind her process of empowerment, how she slowly, steadily, increasingly over the years uncovered her staunch Democrat core. Even when they were liberal Republicans she championed peace, civil rights, and social justice. Her public declaration that she was a "Republican for Johnson" caused my father to lose his campaign for local councilman, but she was undeterred. Within a few years, they were both officially democrats marching in Washington for the end of the Vietnam War.

As this parental metamorphosis occurred, I was elected head cheerleader, winning *best dressed, best-figure, best smile* in the school polls. I was apolitical and utterly uninterested in their new, progressive *Church without Walls* or their fight for women's ordination in the Episcopal Church. I had my own romances, and I knew how to look good on the outside even if inside I was a maze of awkward inhibitions and hesitancies. Mom was brave and she did find her voice politically through social action, but personally, privately, as a woman? No, there she remained deeply hidden.

Dad breaks into my reverie as he shuffles carefully out of the bathroom towards the dining room table. "Would thee like to work with me on that fund raising letter?" he asks hopefully.

"Dad, I can't right now. I'm going to visit Gail." I close my sketch-book and stand to go upstairs to my room. "But we'll talk when we go for a walk this afternoon."

He seems satisfied with this plan, and I climb the stairs slowly. Again, I puzzle at Mom's strange disclosure of this morning. A missionary, a Quaker. Is that what I'm becoming? Am I subconsciously repeating her post-menopausal method of empowerment through social action? I shake my head at the idea. It doesn't ring true. Inside, I'm still a girl who loves beauty and romance and magic. Right?

## A Triumphant Return

It is a strange transition from the warm house of my parents in Portland's burgeoning spring to this bush world where autumn is sneaking up from the ground, yellowing the base of the green grasses. As I drive along the familiar road to Mapusha my American reality seems distant. I will miss the good coffee and endless choices in the Portland supermarkets, but, more deeply I will miss the warm comfort of hanging with Gail in her living room drinking tea and sharing thoughts, dreams, experiences on that substantive level that so nourishes me and is rare in my South African world. I vow to make the drive to Nelspruit more often to see David and Neil who can match me deep for deep, if they so choose.

When I was home, all I could talk about was Mapusha, the women and the world I am coming to know. I had buckets of stories to tell and piles of pictures. Everyone was excited by my excitement and just as surprised as I was that Judy the yoga teacher/counselor had somehow turned into a community volunteer worker in South Africa. A too familiar soft sadness washes through me as I consider my parents, how my presence cheered them and helped my sister Sally out. My absence makes her life harder.

"Let it go," I tell myself firmly for it isn't a choice at the moment. My real life is right here.

I turn my attention to feeling the thrumming vitality of the earth and let my excited anticipation fill me up. How are the women? What is Sampiwe up to these days? And the rug? That's the big question. Did they do it and did they do it right?

I see the door of the studio open and first Gertrude and then all of the women come out onto the steps to greet me. Shaking hands with Regina, Gertrude, Lindy and three Annas I feel the warmth of our reunion. I show them the scarves my mother sent to them, the books for their children, the chocolates I brought from America. Sampiwe comes in the door. Her, I can hug. I squat by her side and she gently strokes my hair and smiles. All is wonderfully festive, but as I look around at the looms and the work in progress I feel a bit apprehensive. I do not see any sign of Alison's 6' by 9' commissioned rug. I walk over to where Gertrude and Regina, wearing their new scarves, are chatting and I ask them about the rug for the white lady in Hazyview.

"Done, gone," says Gertrude with a grin and a swishing hand signaling completion.

"You finished it? Where is it?" I ask, for I had left only a small sketch of the geometric angle motif for the edges of the rug. I very much wanted to see how the design worked in woven wool, if it worked.

"We called the lady and she came and got it and gave us the money for it," said Gertrude, pleased at my level of surprise.

"But, was she happy? Did she like it?"

Gertrude shrugs and I realize that I probably couldn't decipher Alison's response myself so how could Gertrude? I would have to call her and see if she liked the rug, my design, their work. Did I get it right this time?

I know what it took for the women to take my little drawing on the scrap of brown paper and get the wool spun and dyed, get the wall loom warped and then to weave the rug, cut it off the loom, finish the edges, call the customer and complete all of this in under six weeks. I am not only impressed, I know now with certainty that we can work together, that we do have a partnership and that I can completely count on them to do whatever needs to be done to get the job finished. Now, can I hold up my side of the bargain? Can I find enough orders to support them?

We have a new commission from Leslie for a big living-room rug, 3 by 4 meters, a rug as big as the biggest wall loom in the studio. I gaze at the thick beams nailed to the wall, which will provide the tension on the warp strings for this rug. Sitting on an empty wooden table I study the latest design sketch and ponder what the colors should be. I have been sending design sketches by fax back and forth with Leslie. She has an artist's eye and creates elegant and gracious homes. But it is nerve-wracking for me.

Sampiwe brings me back to the moment with a gentle tickle on my arm. I smile and lift her up onto the table where I sit with my untouched colored pencils and paper. I interlace my fingers and repeat slowly the rhyme I am trying to teach her.

"Here is the church, and here is the steeple." I lift my two index fingers to form the church steeple. "Open the door and see all the people."

She laughs at my wiggling fingers and attempts to mimic the church with her small hands. As we continue this play I smile with appreciation of this studio, these women and the very hands-on way my days unfold within their weaving world.

I help Sampiwe form the steeple with her index fingers. Maybe it *is* a missionary role I am playing. Maybe I am living my mother's dream. My world has no men and no pay, but it's such a satisfying reality. It is gritty and real and profoundly touches me. It is a warm, visceral comfort to be with these deeply grounded women in the old studio with the steady whir of the spinning wheel and the tap of the weavers, the soft Tsonga voices.

## Our First Visitors

The women mop the floor and straighten the shelves in preparation for a visit from a touring group of Americans. I wander about agitated, checking my watch, feeling the weight of this visit on my shoulders. The tour leader is a friend of mine and her entourage is from her well off, well-connected California circle. We have hung tapestries in the storeroom and all the women have dressed with special care, covered their good clothes with a stampi (length of cloth) as they move efficiently through their cleaning tasks. The bus is supposed to arrive at 11, and by 11:15 I am tense, my anxiety increasing.

Finally, I see the bus turning awkwardly into the small drive of the mission, bumping over the grated bridge to park in front of the studio. They are here.

Gertrude is the official greeter. She shakes each woman's hand and welcomes each to Mapusha. In the cool shade of the tall studio the Americans crowd around Anna and her spinning wheel. She is bright and engages everyone with her eyes. She loves the attention and the Americans happily snap many pictures of her lean face and bright red turban. I begin to relax watching the interaction, the high level of eagerness and interest between Anna and the guests. Gertrude does a good job, introducing each of the women and speaking briefly about their tasks. Regina and Lindy are at their tapestry looms and they demonstrate the simple over-under basics of weaving and then wow the visitors with the speed of their fingers and the number of little colored balls of wool dangling down from the top of the tapestry. The Mapusha women are shy in a dignified way but I wish I could merge the two groups more completely.

I have an idea. I ask Jane, the tour leader, if her group would like to hear the women sing. They would love it. So I seek out Regina to see what she thinks. Will she gather the women to sing for our guests? Within minutes the whites are arranged on benches and the Mapusha women face us in a semi-circle and begin to sing the song of the co-op. All restraint leaves their bodies as they tap, step and sing together in perfect harmony. Their music fills the room and all sense of separation dissolves.

Gertrude explains that the next song is from their church and in it they are asking the angels to come down to help them. Anna Mbetsi is the lead singer here and her voice soars in the call as the other women respond all reaching up to the heavens with outstretched arms. I feel tears well up and when they launch next into the national anthem, I melt. They finish with a thank you song in which they go around the circle, inviting each guest to shake their hands as they sing their thanks. The visitors are visibly moved and when the singing ends, they move en masse into the storeroom where they buy and buy.

It is all very exciting and I am moving fast, as I help with accounting and answer questions.

"How did you start working with these women? Where do you sell their work? How can we help? Is there AIDS here? Where are the men...?"

Finally, they are herded back onto their bus. We wave wildly as it pulls out the drive.

Gertrude lifts the rands in her hands and announces, "Three thousand four hundred and fifty."

Everyone starts cheering and ulululululululuing and doing spontaneous dance steps. Anna Mduli leads the effort to pick me up on their shoulders.

Later, as I prepare to leave the studio and head home to share our success story with Vicki, I walk over to Regina's loom. She is weaving again but turns to thank me.

I reply, "but it wasn't me."

She nods her head in agreement and points up to the sky. It was something or someone from a larger realm that brought my needs together with the needs of these women she indicates with deep conviction. I have to agree that there is a perfect synchronicity.

The women will eat chicken this Sunday after a gratitude- filled mass. I drive home high with the sense of success for the women of Mapusha and me.

## Inspired by Sinthe

Each morning when I turn onto the familiar, muddy, red dirt road of the co-op, I feel a tingle of eager anticipation. I want to see what Lindy did yesterday afternoon with the center of the triangles on the rug and how Regina handled the leopard's form on the branch of the baobab tree. Often there are conversations with Regina, Gertrude and Emerencia, and I've learned how to ask questions to get answers that help me learn more about their world. My sense of their community is slowly growing.

On Wednesday afternoons the older women of St. Anna come to the mission for a special service. They sit outside the studio on mats with their legs straight in front of them, proudly wearing the purple capes of the Women of St. Anna and pleased to shake my hand each week in greeting.

Today 2-year-old Sinthe is at the studio for some reason. I go to the mat where she lies on her belly, her head lifted to watch the activity around her. She is clearly disabled, though no one has a name for her condition. She cannot speak or walk and her muscles move spasmodically. Usually, when I see her she's tied to someone's back with her too thin, long legs trailing down their side, but today she is on her own. When she sees me coming towards her, her legs and arms start to flail, and she screeches with excitement. I lie down beside her on the blanket and watch her excitement recede into pure pleasure at my proximity. Finding a ball of wool at my side, I roll it towards her but she isn't interested in the ball, she is interested only in me, the white giant with the strange light eyes who is right here beside her. She looks into my eyes and her small hand reaches towards my face. I try my special tongue-popping trick that usually amuses children. But Sinthe doesn't find my sounds entertaining. She would rather bring her hand to my mouth and feel my lips on her skin.

Gertrude's oldest daughter, Susan, has taken over mothering Sinthe since her mother died at her birth. Susan has her own three girls, Eulender, Sandlezi and Amanda, and now Sinthe and her sister Polite. There are no fathers around, and care of Sinthe is a big job.

Gertrude tells me about Susan's small job over at the mission teaching Tsonga to the new Father when suddenly Sinthe breaks into another level of motion and sound. Her whole being vibrates with joy for she has heard her Susan's voice at the door. Susan walks over and lifts the little girl high over her head and all who are watching laugh at Sinthe's delight.

I sit on the bench beside them. She holds Sinthe in her lap, patiently feeding her spoonfuls of porridge as she talks about all the health problems she has with this child, how hard to carry her to town and then to wait in the lines at the hospital. She wishes there was help for the disabled children of the village, she wishes she could do something so that all the mothers wouldn't suffer as she does. "I have a dream," she says softly, her eyes aglitter as she pauses for effect, "to make a home for disabled children."

The idea that this young, vital woman is envisioning something that would help the community tugs on my compassion for the women and children of this village. They have so very few resources other than their own steady feet and hard-working hands. She relates how she struggles to brush Simthe's teeth, and how scared she is that Sinthe will have more seizures in the middle of the night. Sinthe is at the center of Susan's thoughts and actions each day, all day.

At Vicki's lodge that evening, as she bobs in the pool I share my stories from the village, wondering vaguely if there's something I could do for the unemployed young women of the village.

"If you look at it from a business perspective—"

I raise my eyebrows as Vicki pauses, knowing that what is to follow will not mesh with my dreamy web of inspiration.

"It would be best if you could get the weaving co-op on stronger footing and find a way to make a salary for yourself before you got involved in any other projects."

She turns to greet some new guests who have come out from their rooms for the sunset. I listen as she tells them, "You need to listen carefully to hear when the sounds of the day become the sounds of the night." The young European couple is charmed by this notion and venture out with their cameras towards the center of the big lawn, away from all distractions.

She turns her attention back to me. "That's what I'm doing, Vicki," I say. "I'm just watching closely, listening carefully. Watching the women and myself, trying to hear the next steps."

She nods and something softens in her eyes. She does understand the call of the heart, the call to help someone, right some wrong, protect the vulnerable. I watch her climb out of the pool and tie a Kenyan kanga cloth loosely round her waist.

She winces for me when she hears the gossip about my foolhardy ventures from the folks around the reserve. She has never set foot in a therapy room whereas I have spent years, first as the counseled and then as the counselor. I have a familiarity with humiliation that she doesn't share. I fear failing the women much more than I fear wagging tongues. I know how to ride that wave better than most, certainly better than she does, which allows me to take her cautions a little less seriously.

Sitting on the poolside, she says, "I just want you to take care of yourself too."

I nod. I know that's what she's saying and that her proposed course of action has logic behind it. But still, the faces of the young women of the village float in my awareness as we sit watching the changing of the guard, listening as the hum of the insects morphs into the more mysterious whisperings of the night.

## New Beginnings with a New Generation

David and I come up with a plan over the weekend and by the time the sun sets on Sunday, I have written up an email about a proposed apprentice program at Mapusha to send to my whole Portland network. It is safely tucked in the drafts folder on my computer. I must first call a meeting at the studio, put the idea forward and see what the six stalwart co-op members think of my idea of bringing in a new crew, another generation. I have that wonderful swept-up sense, and in the dawn light I set off from the Nelspruit farm towards Rooiboklaagte for a meeting with the women of the cooperative.

By the time I reach the co-op I have a new name for the project: Adopt an Apprentice. I walk through the door and smile at everyone. Regina is at her loom and I immediately take my place at her side and begin to tell her my idea. She is weaving a commissioned geometric tapestry and her fingers move through the white warp strings, intertwining the colored weft yarns. She listens carefully to my words, nodding her head gently. I finish my tale. She looks up at me and with great seriousness says, "It is best that we have a meeting to see what the others have to say."

Regina is always very careful to play down her authority as chairwoman of the co-op. It isn't something I really understand, but I have watched it for months now. She is avoiding trouble, but I can't pin down what that trouble would look like.

At this moment, Emerencia walks through the door. She has been coming to the co-op lately, trying out the craft of weaving, as it bores her to sit at home with no money and nothing to do. Her mother has shown her how to wind the warp from the small cones of white cotton thread on the floor onto the big wooden spool in the corner of the studio. I ask Regina if it would be a good idea to talk to Emerencia and she agrees.

We decide to have a meeting with everyone at 11:30, before the lunch hour. I go to seek out Emerencia's opinion of my bright new idea. She likes to talk and always has opinions. As she winds the thin cotton warp into smooth circles on the spinning spool, I tell her about my conversation with David. I ask what she thinks of bringing on some of the unemployed younger women from the village, teaching them to spin and weave. She is brutally honest.

"But, Judy, these women don't even make money. Why would we want to be part of a falling-down co-op? We have lived and watched for years as they struggled, they haven't done well since the Fathers stopped helping them. Who would want to be part of Mapusha?"

I argue that Mapusha could do well now that people in America like their work. Their rugs are popular. We could have a website, people would come to visit, and we would soon sell things in Johannesburg. I am full of optimism, at my cheerleading best, talking to her because I believe it with all my heart. Mapusha can be a success. I just know it. She seems a bit placated by my words if not fully convinced.

I leave Emerencia to her threads and begin arranging small wooden benches in a circle for our meeting. Regina calls out in her church voice, her big voice, for everyone to leave her weaving and spinning and come over to talk with Judy.

Meetings are always a bit tricky because of the languages. I can be understood by half of the women but only two of them, Regina and Gertrude, can really reply in English. So, I sit on my hands. Regina opens the meeting, and then turns it over to me.

I begin my pitch and soon my hands are out, actively engaged in my description of what I have in mind. I explain the idea of six younger women joining Mapusha, being paid a small salary by sponsors in America for six months as they learn the arts of spinning and weaving. "They will be trained by you to work in the studio."

As my words are translated, I watch Gertrude in particular, for she is the worst at hiding her true feelings. I see her eyes light up. There is a buzz of excitement in our circle and she speaks first. She says in English, "This would be good for Mapusha. It would mean that Mapusha has a life after us."

Regina listens as each woman speaks at length in Tsonga to my proposal. I take in their eyes and their body posture. I listen to their tone and feel their energies. I know pretty quickly that we have a winner here.

Regina puts it into words I can understand, "Judy, we would be very happy if you would help us to grow the cooperative. This is what we want. We thank you."

That's it. It's done. I can put the email into the send box and feel very, very good about the direction in which this, my heart's project, is moving.

# Apprentices Arrive

It's opening day for the Mapusha Apprentice Program and in the bright morning light I feel about as prepared as I know how to be. Beside me on the car seat are Pic 'n Pay plastic bags filled with drawing pads, pristine pencils and sharp edged pink erasers. I have official-looking apprentice agreement forms to be signed and notes and pictures from the American sponsors to be read, a bag of apples, a box of cookies.

Laden with my bags and bundles, I back my way through the door and immediately feel the weight of silence as eight new apprentices sit across the room looking in my direction. They are seated around one of the studio tables, and they watch me closely as I greet the other weavers and come over to their table. I lay down my parcels.

I welcome them one by one and tell them how happy I am that they are here. I go on a bit about the agreement form and tell each a little about her sponsor. Lizbeth is translating for Ambrosia, but the rest of them seem to get the gist of my meaning. Angy, Emerencia and Syndi are the ones most able to meet my gaze so I ask them to pass out the supplies for our first section on design, drawing and painting. It would be good to get away from talking for a while. We will start with a simple drawing exercise. If they are to be designers they need to begin making designs and this should be easy.

Just the other day I stood behind the studio watching a passel of young boys with a couple of pieces of chalk draw complex cars and stunning superheroes on the stained old concrete walls. They seemed so at ease with drawing I don't anticipate any problems here.

Each woman inspects her goods. I ask them to open their pads and decorate the first page any way they like. Syndi picks up a bright orange pencil and plays her fingers around it as her eyes roll up to the sky. Her hair is in a buzz cut and her elegant young face frames big liquid eyes and a wide smile. She dresses with style. Her beauty strikes me. Her skin is dark against the bright yellow of her scoop-necked tee shirt. A shiny wrap-around skirt hugs her slim hips. I suspect she will emerge as a leader in the group.

Poor Wonder looks at me with near desperation, and I just know that she longs to have me give her a bundle of laundry to wash or a floor to scrub, anything but this intimidating blank sheet of paper to be filled by her own creation. Her hair is almost shoulder length, straightened by chemicals. I try to encourage her just to play with the colors. She obligingly picks up a purple crayon and begins making tentative lines on one corner of the paper.

I give them some space, disappearing into the storeroom. Turning my back on the scene I gaze out the window where a herd of cows grazes. I wonder how I am going to get through to these young women.

I hear the words of my teacher from long ago telling me the basis of good communication. "It is like throwing a ball. You need to make sure that your ball is caught."

I'm not at all sure my balls were caught just now. I glance over my shoulder to see how they are doing with their task. It was supposed to be fun, but doesn't seem to be catching on. There is a lack of movement. Maybe it is too much freedom, too much blank white paper. I decide to let them be for a bit and get on with my bookkeeping tasks.

Soon there is a knock on the door and I turn to see Emerencia with her arms crossed over her chest and a frown on her face.

"Judy, maybe you don't know this but it is boys who draw in our culture, not girls. We don't know how to draw. We have never done it."

Inwardly an 'eek' reverberates, but I marshal myself and walk calmly out to the drawing table, look around at the eight pads on the table. Syndi has gamely drawn something that resembles a spear, which looks vaguely familiar. A design on her mother's handbag? Yep, she copied something within sight. I imagine her eyes moving down around the room in search of something and landing there. Well, *that* shows initiative of a sort.

Ambrocia has drawn small simple childlike flowers on her paper which I have seen before in other children's drawings, the stylized flower of all beginning drawers. Again, not a bad start. Beautiful Angy has drawn a teddy bear as though remembered from some coloring book page long ago. She is carefully filling it in with a pink crayon. Emerencia's sheet is nearly blank, as are Emma's, Wonder's and Kamoocho's.

I praise the work that's been done and I begin to question them about gender roles. They can't tell me why only boys draw. Maybe it's because they don't have to sweep the yard or collect the water, or maybe only boys are good at drawing.

I protest.

"In my country there are just as many girl artists as boy artists."

I see a quizzical look on Lizbeth's face and realize she has a translation problem. I ask what she doesn't understand and she tells me it is the word 'Artist'.

"There is no word artist in Tsonga."

"An artist is someone who loves to make things and there are many, many ways to be an artist. You can sing songs, do dances, write books or poems, paint pictures or weave tapestries, many, many different ways."

Watching them trying to understand me, I feel a blank space at the very center of our communications. If my language and accent aren't bad enough, now we are wrestling with a foreign concept. Pretty soon the whole co-op is involved in the controversy and it seems there is no word for artist. Regina saves the day when she comes up with the word 'crafter.'

"These girls are working to be crafters and they will be very good once they learn," she proclaims with calm assurance.

Thus, dispute number one of the Apprentice program is resolved. We forge onwards with apples and cookies and long discussions of who is responsible for cleaning the studio on Friday afternoons.

When lunch hour arrives and all the apprentices wander across the street to the tiny wooden tuck shack to purchase packaged loaves of sliced brown bread, I sit on the front step eating my sandwich and remember my own wretched drawing experience years ago at summer camp. I can still smell the pines of that New Hampshire moment on the broad lodge porch when the teacher asked us to draw our own shoe. I struggled mightily. I can still see the strangely awkward pencil-drawn sneaker on my paper and still remember the feelings of near-tears frustration. I didn't know how to draw my shoe that day and it was years before I picked up a pencil to draw again. Certainly, I want these young women to experience only encouragement and support, but there are big holes in my understanding of them and their culture. After my morning with the younger women, I can see how Regina and Gertrude, Lindy and the three Annas gently fill the holes and gaps between us. They hide, disguise and navigate with such grace, I barely notice. The apprentices extend me no such courtesy; they don't have the confidence of the older women.

I let my eyes rest on the knotted trunk of the old tree shading the yard and try to imagine a design exercise that would allow these eight shy, self-conscious young women to have fun. I look at the usual line of women waiting for water at the well. One woman's head is covered with a yellow fabric while her shirt is a deep blue, her skirt orange, and her stampi is a traditional geometric print. I squint and now the stampis and bandanas of the women in the water lines becomes a design. The fabrics create a mosaic of colorful circles and triangles as they move across the lawn, as they could move across the page.

That's it. The apprentices can play with colored triangles and Elmer's glue. They don't have to draw. They can design. I head back to the storeroom to find scissors and pencils and bright colored paper. I want to be ready when they return to the studio.

## A Fig Jam Moment

Fingering a delicate, palest-of-yellow plumaria petal, I remember two years ago when this tree sent out its sweet scented blossoms. I was recovering from the lumpectomy with a plastic tube draining the incision in my left breast. It was to David and Neil and this farm I turned when I found the lump, and they took on the challenge with great care and practiced efficiency. I became their project, their protégé, their puppy, really, for a time. I stayed in their guesthouse in the hilly outskirts of Nelspruit before and after the surgery and throughout the radiation treatments. They saw me through it all. David cooked thick chicken soups and Neil had me write a long letter to a friend ten years in the future, telling about all the exciting things I'd been doing. They used their combined wit and wisdom as well as David's own 20-year odyssey with the AIDS virus to help me through, and they were proud of my seeming victory.

Their farm is where I go to swallow their inspirational edge, a wild and wonderful nourishment. Vicki is my stalwart Blyde buddy but these men provide the wide, hope-filled view, which I need.

Walking in my flip-flops down the quartz-studded path to their house for Christmas dinner, I breathe in the wide view. It is seven rough kilometers up and down a dirt farm road to their walled fortress on the hill. The thick concrete wall is more for show than safety. It has gaps through which any dog or skellum could wander. They have been building and planting and building and planting on this ever-expanding land of theirs for five years now, and they have five houses and many baobab, leopard, and neem trees planted and gardens of fruit trees to show for it. I look out over the valleys and hills from my perch seeing boulders and wild patches of veld woven together with neatly plowed fields. The elevated, wide perspective that makes me feel especially light and free.

"Well if it isn't Judith B. Miller." David greets me from his stand by the grill where he is impatiently fanning the coals with one hand as he holds a platter of chops and boerwurst in the other.

"And if it isn't the Great White Hope." I quip and he smiles, enjoying the reference to his high status in the AIDS world as a symbol of hope.

"Hello, Alfie," I sink down on the step to pat the big, white male cat, David's beloved buddy.

David is a strange combination. He has fascinated me since I first met him three years ago. He's bright and charismatic and he likes to catch people, shock them, delight and amuse them. One of his favorite activities while living in Palm Beach was to ride through town on a motorcycle with high heels and a blonde wig after not shaving for a week.

Then there are the stories of his smuggling HIV drugs into South Africa, the time he faced down an inspector with the threat that he was a highly contagious AIDS sufferer. Yet, the image that sticks in my head is of David, as a little boy, sneaking out before dawn to give milk to all the feral cats in the neighborhood.

"Happy, happy Christmas and all that. How are you?" he asks with a cheerful smile as he lifts the chops one by one onto the grill.

"I'm great. Feels good to be here for my third Christmas with you guys."

He's busy with the meat placement and I watch his hands - such strong, elegant hands. Like the rest of him they merge a certain feminine sensitivity with the impression of a very masculine strength.

He considers the past three years, the holidays, "I'd say after beating cancer and reviving Mapusha this should be a fig jam moment for you."

I shake my head, puzzled.

"What is a fig jam moment?" I've heard him use the phrase before but never really understood it, as often happens in this world where strange English phrases, Afrikaan's exclamations and African words are thrown into conversations willy-nilly.

"It means 'Fuck I'm great Just ask me," he says and laughs out loud at the shocked reaction on my face. "OK, you keep watch on the grill while I get the veggies." He strides off into the house leaving Alfie and me with the smoking grill.

Stroking Alfie's neck I feel a rough scab. "Have you been fighting again, defending your turf?" He lifts a paw and licks it lovingly. Fuck I'm Great, both David and Alfie seem to be able to put this out and enjoy it far better than I can, not one cell of my being can comfortably rest with this new phrase.

Could Mom say that or some equivalent———minus the fuck of course, which she would never say? No, whether it's Quaker modesty, Episcopalian humility or a woman thing she could not say it, ever. Regina? Nope. Emerencia? Well, Emerencia would want to be able to say it but she couldn't hold it at her center as David does. Alfie has now rolled over to enjoy a light belly rub. I laugh at his pleasure and am reminded of the days when I would tell my yoga students to be like a cat, able to both utterly relax everything and able to bring each muscle to full power in a blink.

David comes back and inspects the state of the chops and strings of browning wurst. I watch him and look for a way to get his brilliant mind to throw some light on my quest to understand FIG JAM in relation to men and women, power and shame. He likes these sorts of inquiries if I can catch the right moment.

He's smoking a cigarette, and though I too love cigarettes I only let myself bum one occasionally, and then it is with a flush of shame.

"Do you smoke during your "Positive Health" trainings?" I ask trying to imagine bumming a cigarette and lighting it up during a break in a yoga class or workshop.

"Yep. It's my one vice and I choose it."

"It doesn't make you feel ashamed at all to be teaching people how to be healthy and happy while doing something everyone knows is suicidal?"

"Nope. My choice, my life. I don't do shame. Been there done that and I won't let it happen again." He is clear and calm on the point as he continues fussing with the meat, seasoning and adjusting. "If someone has a problem with me that is their problem, not mine."

I'm not going to get anything further from him on the subject as he is now fully in host-chef mode. I know he did endure public humiliation as a rebellious, powerful, gay, dyslexic student at a snotty private school in Durban. He doesn't like to go back to those well-remembered shaming moments, but he will answer my questioning on occasion. Obviously, he handled that vulnerability, made a plan and though I would bet it does still reside somewhere deep in his belly, it doesn't seem to affect his actions in the world or his high self-confidence.

I muse on the FIG JAM moment thing and know that though it reflects an attitude that will never be mine it helps me to imagine a way very different from the shrinking stance employed by too many women, which so irks me these days.

The other farm dwellers begin to arrive. Winks, white-haired and suntanned from her work on the gardens and grounds, joins us.

Next Peta and Dave arrive with a plate of Christmas cookies. David shoos us all inside. The meal is ready. He makes beautiful, bounteous plates for each of us, and we carry them into the living room to watch a new British Christmas comedy.

Afterwards, we wipe our brimming eyes, hug, kiss and say goodnight. There are no presents or children, no singing or prayers but it feels good, and I'm happy to be a part of David and Neil's chosen family.

Back at my room up the hill, full of meat and warm feelings of belonging I let myself sigh with the pleasure of how things are unfolding. I am flying by the seat of my pants with Mapusha, but it is alive with possibility. It doesn't make me feel that *I* am great so much as it makes me feel as though *life* is great, and that somehow I have tapped into a good and graceful flow. Turning for one last look over the dark valley I revel in the wonder of the new moon sliver in the star-drenched sky. For the first time in a long time it's one of those perfect moments when all seems right with the world.

# Part Two

## Riding the Waves

# New Year and New Roof

I t is mid-January, the start of the new work year. In the studio, the women are bent over with their rags, buckets and mops, wiping up big puddles of water on the floor. A leaky roof in the summer rains - an inauspicious start to the year. I consider what it would take to get the roof patched.

Slipping off my sandals, I tiptoe barefoot across the wet floor to greet each of the women and exchange 'Happy New Year." Regina suggests we all gather to say prayers for this start of Mapusha's year and, as the fifteen of us stand silently in a circle all I can hear is the drip-dripping of the leaking roof. Gertrude begins a solo prayer in soft Tsonga. I consider how they would feel if I added a prayer for help in mending the roof. They have bigger concerns I decide, more about life and death and food. Also, they are more practiced at ac-cepting whatever is as the will of their god. I ask for help silently, in my own way. I want this old building waterproofed.

Sampiwe begins school today at the Catlego nursery school, a building on the other side of the mission proper. I will miss her play-ful company in the studio, but there is plenty to do as rug orders and commissions have come in from my circle of friends in the States. It isn't a sustainable path forward but I focus on the happy fact that it's happening at all. So far, we have been able to pay each woman a small salary each month.

Gertrude is warping the wall loom with the help of Anna Mduli. I sit, enjoying the rhythm of their cooperation. Anna passes the thin cotton warp thread from the spool up to Gertrude to wrap and hook on a top nail, and then it goes back down to Anna to wrap and hook on a bottom nail — up and down, fast and seamless. As they work I hear the tale of the property on the other side of the mission where Sampiwe is now being schooled. In the '90s, after the mission had stopped supporting their work, a kind Father tried to assist them. He raised money with the help of his sister in Italy and built the building where the creche is housed and a community named the Peanut House. He made the women of Mapusha the trustees of the large fenced property, but they have never been able to do anything other than support the creche minimally and plant their peanuts in the fenced yard of the community building.

The story tickles my curiosity about what goes on beyond the small mission yard where all of my attention has been for the last year. So, as the women settle for lunch I head over to see this land, the school, and the community building. I hear voices of small children before I see them in their windowless, doorless stark room. A smiling old Shangaan woman, who speaks no English, is attending to the twelve kids.

Sampiwe is shy but pleased to see me, and I resolve to find a way to get doors on their creche, and pictures on the walls. I can't help but imagine these lands and buildings fixed up and somehow more useful to the community. I don't know how this could happen but Father Keister's work to strengthen the community was the right action. It needs to go forward somehow, and I can feel my interest beginning to spread out from the weaving studio, following Sampiwe into the community of Rooiboklaagte.

It doesn't take me long to find friends who are happy to help with the costs of the studio roof repair and are excited to help improve the creche. I'm beginning to understand that people in the States want to support this adopted community of mine. They like knowing that they are helping directly and will get a kick out of my pictures of the new roof or the weaver who is weaving their rug. My presence here in Rooiboklaagte gives a personal face and focus to their generosity and it is a heady pleasure for me to be the conduit through which these generosities flow.

Early afternoon on a hot summer's day several weeks later the roofer has been hired and I arrive at the mission yard to check on his progress. Regina and Anna are sitting stiffly on chairs within the fenced confines of the Father's mission yard. Two big dogs race around one of the buildings, growling and yapping at me through the fence. I can feel the tension in the women. It seems all the dogs in South Africa are racist.

"We do not have the key to open the gate and let you in," Regina says with apology on her face.

They can't get up and come over to the fence because of the dogs, which are now pacing the fence, snarling menacingly.

Regina has shed her black clothes after the obligatory year of mourning. She looks fresh and younger in her neat skirt and purple jacket. Anna has on a fancy black bandana and a purple Sunday dress, which means they have been here since the church service ended two hours ago.

"Why are you here? Shouldn't you be home having Sunday lunch with your families?" I ask.

"We are helping the Fathers, protecting their property."

I turn my eyes to the dogs. It doesn't seem fair, but I suppose they are pleased to be of use to the Fathers who live in this compound.

"Where *are* the Fathers?"

"They are doing the mass in other parishes." Regina explains.

It must feel like a privilege to her to have the Fathers live in their village, and even a privilege to spend their Sundays locked into the mission yard with angry dogs. Oh well.

The sound of hammering comes across the yard at the studio.

"Have you spoken with Walter?"

They both shake their heads, and I'm puzzled. The guy is working on their studio. Why wouldn't they take ownership of the situation? I turn to go check on Walter myself, waving to the women and hoping the dogs go back to sleep behind the other building so the women can relax. It makes me wince to consider how my presence riled the dogs actually making their guard job more difficult. I am bumbling my way along in their world the best I can, but I'm humbled daily by the depth of my ignorance.

Walter is high up on the tin roof with bare feet. A spineless ladder of short wooden poles, knocked together haphazardly, leans against the building. Not wanting to distract him, I give him a thumbs-up and walk into the studio to see what I can see. A man working on a friend's house at the reserve recommended him. He is hard to read. It could be he is nice and honest and earnest in his willingness to get the job done right, and it could be that he is a skilled con artist. I don't know.

After my years as a counselor, I pride myself on reading people's eyes and gestures with an instinctual certainty. But, I am learning that my instincts are not universal. They certainly don't cover African men. I am never certain what is really going on beneath what I see. Walter comes quietly in the door and stands with his head bowed, his hands behind his back as if he's waiting for something.

"How are you doing with the roof?" I ask innocently because I really have no idea what it is he could want.

"It is hard work and I am hungry." He says looking up to meet my eyes.

I nod.

"Yes, you must be hungry. How much longer will you need to work?"

He calculates that he has several hours more and somehow I feel as though he is embarrassed for me.

"OK, I'll go talk to Regina and Anna and see if they will be here to check your work before you are paid and can leave."

I'm not really sure how they would check his work without climbing up that inadequate ladder but it seems the right idea. I don't know diddley-squat about building and have little interest in learning. Plus, I'm just not the persnickety inspector type. Regina would be better at that task, I decide, as I walk over as quietly as possible to the fence to speak with the women. When I explain the situation, their biggest concern is getting lunch for Walter. It is beyond discussion. I must go get lunch for him.

Heading off down the road, I'm irritated that we are expected to provide lunch for someone whom we are probably over-paying to fix the roof. A crowd of young men, sitting in the shade of a sheet of tin roof outside the tiny tuck shop greet me with eager playfulness. I can smell the hot grease of the chips they are eating as I step past the rooster strutting about the small yard and into the dark interior. Luckily, there is a loaf of day old bread and a basket of ripe avos, and I relent, buying him a 'cool drink' (soda) as well. After delivering the food to a relieved and thankful Walter and taking some pictures of him perched on the roof with hammer and nails for the donors, I ask Regina if she will take over, as I'm ready to head home.

"No, Judy. I cannot be the boss of Walter." Regina's face is pained, contracted as she makes this admission.

"But Regina, he is working for you. You're the chairwoman of Mapusha and Mapusha hired him to fix their roof. You are his boss."

She shakes her head against my logic and I see, once again, the woman I met on my first visit to the studio, a mélange of anger, shame, and helplessness. I don't want to belabor the point, dig the knife deeper, so I just say, "Oh, O.K. I can be the boss."

I get my book from the car and sit on the steps of the church, out of the dog's sight and within sight of Walter. My attempt to read goes nowhere because my mind is racing with the implications of Regina's inability to act. To my eyes, Regina towers above Walter in power. She radiates a sense of sovereignty. But this is only, I realize, when dealing with women and children in the studio and at the church. Elsewhere, she and the other women rank at the very bottom of the social hierarchy. They are beneath all whites, beneath all who aren't rural and poor, and beneath all men, everywhere. Men, women, power, shame. These are the words that swirl in my head, complete with images and incidents, as I sit shaded from the summer sun by the church. These powerless people, I think with despair, are the women I'm hoping can learn to be entrepreneurs.

Here in the mission yard I run my hands through my hair, stroking my head in hopes of awakening a new angle, a new approach to the disempowered women of the village. Just the feel of my hair, now long enough to cut, lifts my spirits. For years my straight brown hair was long, often carelessly clipped on top of my head or loose and swinging around. After the dismal hair experience of the chemo year, now, when I get my hair cut in Hoedspruit I watch in the mirror as he clips the almost curly hairs into a spiky irreverent shape. It's a new look. It's a new life, and change is possible, which will have to suffice as my big picture moment for the day. Hair grows and change happens.

Walter finishes at last and we shake hands. I give him an envelope with the correct number of 100-rand notes. He promises to come back right away if there are any problems, any problems at all. I watch him walk down the drive with a proud, jaunty gait. The metallic clink of the mission gate startles me, and turning I see Regina and Anna exiting their cage. They are free and we say goodbye quickly. Each of us is eager to be home.

"Fambagathe." Travel well.

"Salagathe." Be well.

## Banking with Regina and Gertrude

It is the last Thursday of the month. There is money in the Mapusha bank account. Regina and Lindy are in the storeroom calculating salaries and I am waiting to be the chauffeur for the Hoedspruit bank run. I sit on a table with my legs swinging off the floor and watch Ambrocia weave. She wears a tan hat with a short rim, the type of hat I would imagine on a skinny white male golfer. She seems to be concentrating on her tapestry but I don't sense the same trance that emanates from Regina, Lindy and Gertrude when they sit before the loom. Maybe it comes with time, though I remember sitting on the rug before my homemade Navaho loom and losing everything beyond the threads before me, the rhythm of the colors and their interplay on the warp.

During that summer in Oregon I was living with Joe before we were married. We built my simple frame loom together, and while he worked I spent my days weaving. He would return from his work pouring concrete for swimming pools and invariably startle me. He would laugh and I'd drop my threads and hug his deliciously-worked, warm body. We would head for the tennis court or the track or the bedroom. It was a love filled summer of weaving and u-pick raspberries, blueberries, black berries. We ran down mountains and camped besides streams and played tennis on the long warm evenings. It was a record year of consecutive sunny days in Oregon that summer, over 80 in a row, and I can still see Joe in his favorite red gym shorts jogging on the track after our tennis with his long wavy brown hair and deeply tanned torso. Regina and Lindy emerge and I shake my head returning to the present.

We are ready to go. Gertrude and Regina both wear their city shoes and shirtwaist dresses, the common dress style in Acornhoek. They carefully carry their handbags. Gertrude's dress is brown and yellow in a fish scale pattern. She has on the headscarf that my mother sent as a present, and she is pleased, nodding her head with a big smile when I notice. Regina's dress is green and white with apples dancing across the simple bodice and gathered skirt. A black scarf is draped over her shoulder which I have learned is the modern equivalent of traditional Shangaan dress and always involves a piece of fabric knotted at one shoulder. She holds a detailed list with names and numbers and even the necessary breakdown of denominations into fifty or hundred rand notes. Showing me the total on her paper, she straightens with the weight of her responsibilities and then carefully climbs into the back seat while Gertrude takes her turn in the front.

I enjoy my monthly rides with these two, for it is my chance to ask questions and sound them out on problems, ideas. Whoever sits in the front seat gets to try to understand my queries and answer as best she can.

"How do you think the apprentices are doing?" I immediately ask Gertrude, while I negotiate a family of goats who have been scarfing up cabbage leaves. They still have green scallops hanging from their lips as they cross the road.

"It is good. They are trying and they are learning," she responds, nodding her head and gently tapping her fingers on the worn purse in her lap.

I nod, consider, and then ask if she would yell the same question back to Regina. After some fast-paced Tsonga going back and forth across the seat, I get the same answer from Regina, via Gertrude,

"She says it is good."

Oh, for the days back in Portland, driving along with Gail, discussing in detail the process of our clients, putting our heads together to come up with an insight or a larger understanding. But, that is not my lot here. I consider what a conversation with Gail would be if we could discuss Syndi and Emerencia, Angy, Ambrocia and Wonder as I turn at the light leaving the bustling street life of the township behind. we begin the fast portion of the 25-kilometer drive to Hoedspruit.

Soon, Gertrude exclaims and points to a family of warthogs who have slipped through the fence of the game reserve to eat the grass growing on the side of the road. It is impossible not to smile at these strange, prehistoric, horned heads and tails sticking like little antennae, straight up in a row. I give up on any talk or thought of the apprentices and just enjoy the ride through the spring bushveld, asking Gertrude about her grandchildren, her husband, and her garden.

I can see the line snaking out of the bank as we pull into the lot. This is where my American impatience is severely tested. Regina and Gertrude take their places patiently at the rear of the slow-moving line. I go next door for samosas, and pop back to see that they have moved 10 feet. I tell them I am going to get tea and sugar for the coop. A half hour later, they are getting close to the teller's window. I join them in the queue and see if I can stand just as still, just as solid as Gertrude. There is a child strapped on the back of the woman in front of me, and I start playing peek-a-boo with the little girl who gets spooked and burrows her face into her mother's back.

Finally, it is done. Regina has carefully recounted the pile of bills and Gertrude has put the pile in a cloth bag, the cloth bag in a paper bag and the paper bag in her shoulder bag before exiting the double-doored bank. This is all calculated to fool the local thieves who might think there is nothing of value in a paper bag. We climb back into the hot car and I offer them each a greasy samosa wrapped in gray paper from the Indian shop on the corner.

Regina is in the front seat this time and I compliment her on her dress. When I first met her she was dressed all in black. She was upset, sad and angry that first day, and I am still curious about her feelings around the death of her husband. I decide to ask her about it and see if her answer helps me to understand any better how she looked at our initial meeting. She was sad but it was such an angry sad. What was that anger about?

"I remember when I met you, you only wore black," I say and glance over to see if I can go further or if the doors have shut.

"Yes," she says. The Shangaan tradition, she tells me, calls for black clothes and only one tin plate to eat from for a whole year following a husband's death. And you must sit on the floor away from others. No parties, and no friends unless they, too, are widows.

She is generous with her information about her culture. I tell her that widows in India sometimes burn themselves on their husbands' funeral pyres.

She looks straight out the front window and says with a steady voice, "My husband died to me many years before he died. He was dead to me when he left me. When he was very sick and came back to the village to die, his sister wanted me to care for him but I said, "No, I will see him again when he is dead."

I am shocked at her vehemence, and I can sense the outrage she still feels at his betrayal, the humiliation of his abandonment. When she saw his corpse at the funeral it was the first time she had seen him in years. For a year she had to publicly mourn this man.

Joe comes to mind once again, the night he took me out for a romantic dinner and gave me a bottle of prescription pills for the gonorrhea he "picked up" on his hunt to find a child we could adopt in Guatemala.

"Instead of a child I have your wretched, rotten, gross disease and I have to take these fucking pills?" Yes, I knew the outrage of betrayal and humiliation. But no one made me wear black when he left.

We are waiting at the single stop sign in the center of town and I gaze out over the many women walking on the roadside, standing by the vegetable stands. So much black, so many capes of black and cloaks bandanas, dresses of black moving through the crowd.

"Did he die of AIDS?" I ask.

There is a long beat of silence in the car and finally she says, "He lived as though he should die of AIDS."

I nod and can feel my heart beating rapidly in my chest. I have never before dared say the word AIDS. No one speaks of AIDS here although David swears the infection rate in the village is probably as high as 35%. I turn into the driveway of the mission and park beneath the amarula tree. Regina and Gertrude go in but I sit for a bit in the warm car.

I have an inkling of an understanding of how Regina felt at the death of her husband and the cultural strictures, but the tone of her voice held more. I begin to grasp why AIDS is such a secret here. Her husband grew up in her village and went to the same Catholic school as she and all the others. She married him both by jumping the broom in the cultural tradition and in a service at the Catholic Church. And he had left her for another woman. He had broken his word to her and to God. He was a sinner. In her eyes, AIDS and sinning are entwined, almost synonymous. AIDS and sin and secrecy and shame are all mushed together in one big messy globule trying to hide itself. But hiding is hard in a close-knit village and the AIDS death comes painfully, slowly.

In the studio I wander amongst the looms, greet the apprentices and wait with them as Regina and Lindy ready the worn envelopes that are distributed each month. Each has the name of a different woman printed in faded ink. We had to get new envelopes to hold the apprentice's small monthly wages. There is even an envelope with my name carefully printed upon it. I am still mulling over my conversation with Regina as I sit watching the apprentices. There is a method to everything and I'm not surprised when it is me they call in first to receive my pay. Regina hands me my envelope with the rand equivalent of gas money for the month and thanks me.

## Mapusha's Hoedspruit Debut

I need to get these designs done as well as get things together for the show this weekend at the celebratory opening of the stylish new shopping center in Hoedspruit. Painting in the triangles of the design on the brown butcher-block paper, I mentally tick off what we will need to make this weekend's event, our official Hoedspruit debut, a success.

Heidi, the editor of the local newspaper, has taken Mapusha into her brood of good causes and proposed that we display our woven goods in the tourist information shop at the new mall. She is blonde and solid and always flying around town in her van with one or all three of her blonde children and a nanny trailing behind her as she covers events for the paper. Together we have constructed a teepee of poles encircled with twine to be the centerpiece in the shop. We hope it will be a playful way to display the co-op's tapestries.

Syndi and Emerencia are coming to demonstrate weaving and spinning on the wooden decking outside the thatched shop and I am confident of both their social skills and their English. Much of the work to be displayed is by the apprentices, and I look forward to some useful feedback for them as well as sales to bolster the co-op's bank account. Heidi has made me feel like the new kid at school who has finally found a friend. We have had fun envisioning together how to publicize the co-op and I am buoyed at her willingness to help me champion Mapusha.

Washing out my paintbrush I squint at the design on the table and try to envision what it will feel like as a woolen weaving on the floor. I will give it to Gertrude tomorrow and she will begin to dye the wool and warp the loom to make this paper design into a rug. It has triangles of deep red-orange against a background of the yellows, grays, and pale greens of the winter bushveld. Time for bed, as tomorrow will be a full day of prep for the show at the cooperative. Walking to my rondavel in the light of the full moon, I laugh to consider that my cheerleading efforts with the apprentices tomorrow will be just another round of what began decades earlier in a pleated green skirt with pom-poms in front of the football stands at Welsh Valley Junior High school.

We have tools and tapestries to gather, pieces to label and signs to make. Going over the list of to-dos on the way to the co-op, I decide I will have to talk with the girls about sales and receipts, our email list. I wish with a pang that they would be as excited as I am at the opportunity we have on Saturday. Maybe I could help them envision what a difference it would make to have the support of the local white community rather than count on friends in distant America. Emerencia and Syndi seemed particularly reticent about the whole affair yesterday, but I will try again today.

The girls are being dutiful if not exactly efficient with their assigned tasks, but there is no heart, no fun or anticipatory excitement in the work. I sit on my favorite table and watch Emerencia slowly sewing our shiny, new labels onto each of the tapestries in the pile that is bound for Hoedspruit. She is easy to read. I always know if she is up or down, inward focused or outward. But to understand what caused a mood swing is much more of a challenge. Syndi on the other hand has perfected a pleasing, helpful style but I never really know how deep it goes. I always have the feeling that something else is going on in her mind even as she mouths sweet phrases.

Why is the younger generation so much harder to work with than their mothers and aunties? Gertrude, Regina, Lindy and the three Anna's just do their work in the best way they know how day in and day out. They are unfailingly courteous and they have fun besides. The younger bunch seems more like a high school clique when they sit together eating lunch, so many moods and undercurrents, insecurities and so much hidden. How much of this comes from growing up in a village under Apartheid?

I have an idea to pep them up. "Emerencia, would Sampiwe like to come with us tomorrow?" I turn to include Syndi. "And Preference could come, too?" Preference is a little older than five-year-old Sampiwe but they are neighbors, and go to Sunday school together. They would be excited at the adventure, I'm sure of it.

Emerencia stops sewing and lifts her head to face me. "We never go to Hoedspruit. That is the Boers' town and I am worried for Sampiwe to be there."

"You mean when you grew up blacks weren't allowed in Hoedspruit?" I want to understand if her complaint is part of a generalized chip on her shoulder or a real worry with teeth.

"There was nothing for us there. We weren't welcome and we didn't go there."

But, isn't it the job now to let go of that past, I think, and shouldn't she be working to help Sampiwe grow up in a different reality? How can I say this to these young women without sounding hopelessly naive?

I speak earnestly. "But Emerencia, it's different now. One of the ministers at the dedication will be a black man from Acornhoek, and Heidi is proud to have Mapusha in her store. We need to show Hoedspruit who we are. We need to act as if there aren't the same old boundaries and barriers between us anymore. Don't you think Syndi?"

Emerencia isn't convinced, but Syndi is quick to pick up the beat. "Yes, we will pray to God to help us be strong and teach the Afrikaners' that we are beautiful."

I laugh and begin to tease them about being beautiful. I want to encourage them to feel challenged by this event, see it as an opportunity for that heady sensation of success. Syndi convinces Emerencia to let the children come with us and they continue their work with more enthusiasm as I pack the car.

The next morning no one's in sight when I pull up outside the locked weaving studio at our pre-arranged meeting time of 8 a.m., so I have time to sit under a tree in the silence of the mission yard and consider the day ahead. Doubts assail me from all corners. I put on my cheerleader persona for Emerencia and Syndi yesterday, but Hoedspruit scares me a little, too.

When I first came to Hoedspruit six years ago the town center consisted of a gas station and a small strip of brick buildings, which included a slower-than-molasses bank and a meagerly stocked grocery store. It was a town for the Afrikaner farmers of the fertile valley. But now, I argue with my doubts. The English speakers are creeping in. All those five-star private game lodges have popped up and the new Southern Cross School is pulling in the kind of people who would want to help Mapusha. Heidi is deeply involved with this new private school with an emphasis on ecology and environmental education. Hoedspruit is changing. This shopping mall reflects the new influences, and caters to more sophisticated shoppers.

I sigh. In truth, even with hopeful new residents and modern build-ings in Hoedspruit, the anxiety and separations bred by five decades of Apartheid won't just evaporate.

Another fear emerges when I envision our teepee of string fes-tooned with the apprentices' bright tapestries. I know in my design-er bones that the display and the weavings look crude and wrong on this hot sunny spring day. Wool is not compatible with the heat of the bush. Wool and lowveld just don't match. I know it, and I suspect that the primitive tapestries of the apprentices are not going to be appreciated by the town-folks.

Just as I am about to combine my doubts about our audience with my doubts about our display, four figures walk up towards the gate at the bottom of the yard; two tall, two small. As they approach I see that Syndi isn't there. She has sent her sister Kamocho. "Dang her!" While Syndi is the personification of charm and beauty, her younger sister wears a habitually grumpy look and does not like speaking English. I cannot imagine how I am going to imbue her with the cheerful, friendly, welcoming spirit called for today.

I ask what happened to Syndi as soon as they walk up to the car. "She is sick with the flu." says Emerencia with a shrug. She's too politic to disparage her peer publicly, but her body language lets me know she is not totally behind this tale. I welcome Kamoocho and tell her she has a big job, she has to smile all day long. She can't help but laugh and I see she is a little bit excited herself. Sampiwe is dressed to the hilt with red bows in her pigtailed hair. She has bor-rowed her grandmother's special Mary bracelet for the day and the hooded Madonna is repeated on tiles around her small wrist. She skips with excitement alongside her friend Preference, who looks handsome, decked out in a smart, ironed white shirt.

"Okay, here we go on an adventure!" I say with enthusiasm and I push the doubts out of my mind as I open the door to let my crew into the car. Emerencia is designated front seat passenger and Kamoocho sits with the children in the back. It is a treat for them to be in a private car, and they wave happily at the kids on the side of the dirt road they are used to walking themselves.

When we arrive at the Komogela center, I laugh to see a crew of workers still working up on the fancy thatch at the arched entrance. There must be some problem, or maybe they are just completing it. We unload the car but the tourist shop is chaotic and there is a crowd surrounding Heidi, peppering her with problems and questions. I decide the best course of action is to go outside and begin setting up the small frame loom for Emerencia and the spinning wheel for Kamoocho on the deck, but the deck isn't really wide enough for two crafters and their equipment and the flow of traffic. The only solution here is to place Emerencia and Kamoocho at an awkward angle to the pedestrians.

There is a way, I've noticed, that black women who are hired as nannies to white African children are experts at being there but not there. They've perfected invisibility. I don't want Emerencia and Kamoocho to assume the invisible stance. It is the antithesis of empowerment. And yet, I know it takes grit to keep smiling as people pass you by again and again. It feels to me like Emerencia and Kamoocho have circumstances stacked against them. I'm beginning to get jittery.

Sampiwe and Preference are fine, excited by all the activity in this new place. I suggest they walk around the whole deck of the shopping center and see everything. They grab each other's hand and set off with bright eyes. Turning my attention to the display, I'm disheartened to see that in the hustle and bustle some of the tapestries have fallen to the floor and some are crooked on their strings. The whole thing looks amateurish, and my belly tightens in anticipation of humiliation to come. It isn't my humiliation but theirs that makes me tense. Oh, how I wish I were one of those people who has everything perfectly prepared, one basket for all necessary tools and one for paperwork, everything neatly enveloped and labeled. Heidi is too much like me, a visionary with a heart but not a bastion of orderly planning. I re-pin and rearrange the best I can, and then walk outside to the center of the parking lot to survey the scene.

My cell phone rings. Reaching into my voluminous shoulder bag I find it. It is a woman I know a bit, an Afrikaans businesswoman who has five exclusive weaving shops in all the top spots throughout South Africa and today is opening the sixth at the Kamogela Mall. Her English is heavily accented but I quickly grasp the fact that she is mad and she is mad at me.

She tells me that the article in the paper about the Mapusha Weavers is unfair to her store. She, too, has weavings for sale only she doesn't have the ear of the local paper. Why hadn't I considered her store?

I'm completely shocked and barely know what to say.

"But, but, but Peta," I work hard to break into her torrent of words. "Our weaving is tapestry and the apprentices are new. You can't compare our tiny cooperative to your very exclusive stores."

She can and she does. She feels very badly treated by me and she has to go.

I stand with the phone in my hand. Closing my eyes I try to get a grip on myself so I don't cry, not here, not now. How can she consider it a competition when hers is a successful for-profit business backed by substantial investors. Mapusha is a tiny little township business with no backers and pathetic salaries. It doesn't make any sense. But maybe she is saying that I betrayed her by aligning with the blacks instead of with her. Perhaps Mapusha represents the black world that threatens the safety and prosperity of her white world. I feel like I am falling down a rabbit hole though I still stand with the phone clutched in my hand.

I understand it all in a flash. My Mapusha friends are not going to get any support from this town, for they are perceived as the victors. Their side won. It isn't going to be like an event in Portland where people are inspired by the women of the cooperative and want to help and support them. I fumble in my bag for my sunglasses and push them on as tears stream down my face. No one speaks to me, but they look at me standing there alone in the middle of the square, crying.

I bite my lip gently to stop the tears. Sampiwe and Preference are walking towards me with big smiles. I don't want to cry in front of them. I remember a young village boy telling me proudly that he didn't cry at his brother's funeral. Crying is not respected in the black world, or in the white.

We walk together towards the Mapusha display where I look at Emerencia weaving away with concentration. She isn't going to look up at the people passing by her and I understand. I don't blame her. Kamoocho has her usual slight grimace as she spins but there is ferocity to the blankness of her gaze as she pedals the spinning wheel. She was excited this morning. One hour into the event she already knows she will be less than nothing to the people here. She isn't going to try again. I stand beside them with my sunglasses still hiding my swollen eyes and say nothing. I can feel their hurt in my heart. They don't want to be seen because being who they are is not good enough.

There is a new Wimpy's at the other side of the mall and I get some money out of my wallet and suggest that all four of them have lunch there. My treat. They will be better off as part of the crowd, I hope. Emerencia and Kamoocho both look at me with grateful smiles. They head off and I sit down beside the spinning wheel, trying to don the invisible cloak myself, keeping my sunglasses on.

I hear English being spoken in the shop. I peek in and see the back of a woman who owns a plot at the reserve. Vicki told me she did interior design, and I had hoped that she might be able to help me with designs and marketing for the upscale world. With one glance I see her response. She holds one of Lizbeth's weavings and her mouth is set in a grimace. I shrink hearing her words of distain for the work. She is English, and supposed to be my ally. My hope for help from the locals doesn't look promising.

Vicki appears just then, takes my arm and brings me into the store to meet her friend the interior designer. We shake hands and she says bluntly, "Nothing the women are doing is sellable. If you come up with something new let me know." I agree with a nod and she moves on. I turn and just look at Vicki.

"No encouragement, no ideas, no support, nothing positive, nothing." I whisper heatedly.

She gets it and tries to calm me as I vow to never, ever tell the apprentices what she said, absolutely never. It would make them feel smaller. I have moved from shattered to pissed, but both Vicki and I know this is not the place for me to vent.

"Come down to the lodge when you get home. We'll talk."

I abandon the teepee of tapestries and wander off into the crowd. Someone is speaking on a stage at the other side of the lot and as I approach I see it is a black man. He is offering prayers for this beautiful new mall.

"May it serve to unite the peoples of Hoedspruit and beyond," he cries out in his deep, rich preacher's voice.

## Ramani Visits

Ramani is coming. She's coming with her very own California 'psychodramatic workshop' designed, at my urging, to help spark the apprentice's empowerment process, such as it is. I smile to imagine the meeting of my red-haired dynamo friend with the women of Mapusha.

Syndi sees the bakkie turn into the driveway first and raises the call. Her whole posture of barely restrained enthusiasm asks if she can greet our guest and I wave my hand for her to go, go. The others stay seated but their eyes are glued to the door. I join Syndi outside and smile to see Ramani's bright orange kinks spiking out from beneath her cowboy hat as she emerges from her white bakkie. She was born and raised in Texas and her twang is evident,

"Hey, Hey, How ya'll doing?"

She wears a fuchsia tee-shirt with the bejeweled face of an Indian goddess outlined in sparkles, and dripping with plastic globules. Syndi's smile widens as she is swept up in Ramani's arm on the way to the door. They walk into the cool shade of the studio together and Ramani waves to all the women. Her eyes take in the large room, the older women perched on their stools, their hands moving the threads, while the younger women, hands unmoving, watch her. She is onstage, center spot and she does it well with command energy and enthusiasm, ready to go. Ramani is always ready to go.

Soon, we are in the storeroom and she is explaining to the girls that no, she doesn't want to know their names, she wants to see their names. She demonstrates who she is with a diagonal swing of her right arm up and a dramatic left knee half drop that turns her body into a veritable lightening strike. Each girl is to show the group their name in a gesture. This is the kind of thing that makes me cringe and I am relieved to be sitting quietly in the observer chair, neither student, nor teacher.

My first time on stage was in an elementary school play. I had five lines to speak and a banana to eat. I actually wet myself with fear when it was my turn to go on stage.

Ramani asks for a volunteer, and up goes Syndi's hand without a moment of hesitation. She stands eager and ready. Once there is quiet in the room and all eyes are upon her she goes into a fighting stance with slim arms raised, biceps flexed and fists on high. Ramani leads everyone in a cheer for Syndi and she returns to her seat radiating pleasure. Emerencia jumps up next and she, quietly as though she were in church, brings her hands together at her heart and kneels on the floor. Interesting choice for my most contentious apprentice. But she is one for surprises. I sense an age-old tension between her and Syndi. If Syndi is the fighter, Emerencia must be her opposite, the nun.

It's Ambrocia who really gets things going when she rises slowly, moves to the center spot and with a smile, turns her back to the group and moves her ample hips in a saucy swag. I've watched crowds on the sidewalk gather round a dancer moving to loud gospel or pop music piped through crackly speakers on the storefront. Always, all action is centered in the hips, in the butt. Slow or fast it is always sexy. Here in Africa, breasts aren't sexy, they are the province of babies.

Soon, Ramani has them doing their gestures in time to the music, her song, her singing, her CD playing on the boom box she brought. She leads the group on and now they are exchanging gestures, building their gestures together into a human sculpture, creating new gestures. The room is alive with movement, laughter and fun.

Watching Ramani orchestrate this group reminds me of my first trip to Africa, sitting in a community hall having a sing fest with a group of Baptist women who were having a retreat in their own center down the hill from ours. I had just met Ramani on this Meditation for Peace tour to our teacher's homeland, South Africa. Seventeen of us landed in Johannesburg and immediately were ferried to our retreat center in the red-rocked hills outside the city. We shared a dining room with these radiant black Baptist women who, even in the cafeteria lines with trays in their hands, could not stop singing. I was agog with the thrill and wonder and beauty of it all and when I expressed my appreciation to the woman next to me in line for her hot dog, she asked if our group wouldn't come have a sing along with them.

We were all eager to go and filed into the community meeting room after dinner. If you have never been in a room with over a dozen African women singing their faith it would be hard to imagine the depth of heart that happens. These women in their fancy church dresses with low heels and big hats serenaded us with hymns, hand clapping and arms to the heavens alleluias. Then, they asked us to sing for them and there was an awkward silence as we all looked around among our white group of meditators for someone who could do something. It was Ramani to the rescue and her vivacious lead kept us from abject failure though our voices at their reedy best were a teeny, weeny, itsy bitsy prayer compared to our Baptist counterparts.

Sampiwe sticks her small, close-cropped head through the doorway, unable to resist at least seeing what the fun emanating from the usually silent storeroom is all about. When she sees her mother and the others all doing a complex dance step she lets her school backpack slide from her shoulders, steps out of her sandals and joins the end of the line. Sure enough, she picks up the step and is clapping along before I can get my camera out of the case and focused.

I wander on the outskirts of the action with my camera, which makes everyone even more of a ham. Emerencia and Angy do a giggly, sultry pose for me and Ambrocia joins Kamoocho, Wonder and Emma in a beaming but studied embrace. I watch Syndi speaking earnestly with Ramani and I have the sense that something will come of this. Ramani has a soft heart, and she has inherited a portion of her grandfather's oil well in Texas. She has a big vision, and I have watched her give and give, and though it doesn't always work out, it is part of her fast-moving, ever-creative propulsion onwards.

She is wrapping things up now and everyone is seated, listening as she tells them to dream big. We begin to take our leave after Ramani scoops up some rugs for her new home and promises to return soon, shaking her finger at the girls with mock ferocity, daring them to live their gestures, to be all they can be. We hug at the fun of it all, another good time shared by the two of us in South Africa. We head out, back to the reserve in our separate vehicles.

As the day's sun weakens, creating long intricate shadow patterns on the mountains, I follow her bakkie down the road and wonder what impact this experience with Ramani will have upon the girls. It was so easy for them to catch her flavor, imitate her body-centered games, almost too easy. We have such different styles and I could no more create a drama than she could move a crowd with her own vulnerability.

Once, several years ago, she came to Portland to help raise money for an orphan-filled farm with her new one woman show, "Kali's Follies." It was a 90-minute monologue-montage, created for her transpersonal doctoral program. It covered the history of women complete with props and costumes and many personas. I was to introduce the show and speak briefly about the AIDS orphans in Africa and Sophie's farm. As the crowd filed in, behind stage where we waited, all she could say to me over and over was "No crying Judy, just don't cry."

I managed not to cry that night but my presentation style was and is the only way I know how to stand in front of a crowd, trying to be transparent and honest, letting my heart lead. She has the glitz and the edges and the sheer force to make things happen, but will anything be different tomorrow? For six months now I have been working, cajoling, attempting to inspire and enliven these eight young Rooibok women, and still a line of connection eludes me. Too often I have the sense of being a teacher at the front of the room, being obeyed. I lack the connection I have with the older women. Did she create a synapse today that will hold? If so, can I keep it alive?

## Anna Mduli Needs Help

Rushed and pushed and trying to get everything together for my next departure to Portland in two weeks, I raced out of the house with no lunch. On the road to the co-op I stop at my favorite little roadside stand. Gladys, the owner, comes at a run from her house across the street when she sees my car pull up under her tree. Wearing traditional cotton cloth wrapped and tucked around her waist she runs with small steps. Her cheerful face, framed by a bright yellow bandana, bends to my window and I relax into her warm presence. We exchange words about the weather. I dig out change for a bag of boiled peanuts and a bunch of bananas. She pockets the change, bowing slightly with a smile and I go on my way.

As I turn into the mission, making a mental list of all that needs to be accomplished today, I see Anna Mduli's son, Vusi, sitting on the outside step of the studio. His form is long and slim like his mother's, his tee shirt is old and his rumpled khaki pants are beltless. He stands as I approach. He is waiting for me.

"My mother she would like to speak to you, only you." His teenage face is creased with worry. Clumsy with nerves I drop my packages inside the studio and tell Regina where I am going. She nods her head but looks grave. My tension increases as I follow Vusi down the path to their home. The summer rains have been good. The fields on either side are vibrant spring-green. The mealies are tall, and the birds sing as we pass beneath a big old tree. Vusi's silence is ominous, usually he is eager to speak English with me. My mind is a high-pitched hum. I have never before been summoned to one of the women's homes. I have never even been inside Anna's.

We pass Regina's house with its masses of purple bougainvillea spilling over the wire fence, and I know that the big house with the wire fence and the unraked yard down the rutted road is Anna's. There is no neat garden there, for Anna has been too weak to work the earth. Her husband died before I appeared, but I know he worked in the mines. The size of the house means that once Anna's family was comparatively well off. She has three sons but only Vusi still lives at home.

He swings the crooked fence open and walks with his head down as I follow him through the wooden front door. After the bright sunshine it is dark inside, but as my eyes adjust I see a pallet in the corner of the big rectangular room.

Anna lies on the pallet. Her body barely makes a ripple under the blanket, and her eyes seem huge in her thin, thin face. They are fixed on me with intensity. I kneel by the bed and greet her. Her eyes fill with tears and she whispers in the English she barely knows, "HIV positive."

I sit back on my heels, as the loud messy sobs of Vusi behind me fill the room. I can feel the ache of fear and despair in Anna's eyes deep in my heart. I fumble internally as all the words and stats from David and Neil's work with HIV flow through my mind, but I know that is not the essence of what she needs. I ask Vusi to help me, translate for his mother. I tell her we will fight this, that we can do it together.

Telling her of my own battle with illness when I had to find my will to fight, I try to inspire Anna to have courage. I promise to come back next week before I go to the States and I tell her I will be "full, big, fat with information" for her. I will bring her whatever David and Neil recommend, and she, too, must begin to fight. She must ask her God for help, and go back to the clinic, and eat meat, and not eat sugar, and ask for help, and believe that she can win.

"Anna, may I tell Regina and the others at the co-op?"

She looks down, away from me and is silent for a moment.

"They are your friends, Anna, and they will support you. We must all make a team to give you the power to win."

Her dark eyes look into mine and though she is dubious, she nods agreement.

I bid Anna goodbye, holding her skeletal hand between mine and repeat my words of fight and power and hope. Vusi walks me to the gate and thanks me and, again, I do my best to fill him with hope, and then slowly begin my walk back to the co-op. The harsh reality of Anna's condition awakens me. All the colors are brighter, all the sounds a little more distinct.

I pass an old woman who totes a load of wood on her head, and consider what it takes for her to walk at least a mile to where there are no houses and thus still wood to be foraged from the bush. It must be a three or four hour journey she has just completed and she probably has only enough wood for a morning and an evening fire, no more. I greet her and give a thumbs-up. She smiles. A few strands of wobbly wire make up the clothesline where a slight, young woman is hanging small, very worn clothes to dry. I wave at her and say "Hello!" to her two children, who run to hide behind her skirts in response. Everything and everyone here looks to need so much. Anna's longing eyes fastened onto me seem to loom over everything. There is so much need, so much poverty, so much to do here. The grasses move in the breeze and an eagle circles high in the sky.

At last I am inside the studio, the cool shade of the high-ceilinged room with the whir of the spinning wheel comforts me. Without preamble I tell Regina that Anna is HIV positive and needs our support. And she, without missing a beat, replies,

"Yes, we will all support Anna. At church we always hear to treat our neighbors as Jesus would and we will do it. It does not matter that she is HIV+."

Relief trickles through me. While no one speaks of AIDS in this world, Regina will lead the women of Mapusha in a loving response, helping their friend without judgment.

Gertrude is too high up for me to have this conversation, so I climb up and stand on the table to talk to her. Her eyes are full of concern as I tell her of Anna's condition but there is no fear, no retreat from the news. She nods her head and again I am reassured that the cooperative will work together to help Anna. Gertrude continues to weave and I watch her fingers plying the white warp threads.

"What about getting tested?" I ask.

She shrugs.

I climb back down and go over to the corner where I so hastily dropped my things earlier. As I dig for my water bottle, I consider the apprentices. Emerencia and Angy are winding wool together and chatting. I watch them as I drink my water. They are so beautiful with their smooth skin, white teeth, and curved bodies. They are twenty-seven years old, which means they are smack dab in the most likely to be infected age group. Angy's brother is sick these days, so are Syndi and Kamoocho's brothers. They say it is the flu, but it goes on and on. I remember Anna's face on the pallet this morning again, and that does it. I will dare to bring up the fraught topic of testing. I walk over to the table and just state it simply.

"Anna is sick, she is HIV+."

Lizbeth, right in front of me, doesn't look down but her eyes take on a certain blankness, a glaze. The walls go up, and for a second I catch a tactile sense of being caught, as these young women are, by the stealthy pandemic imploding in their village.

Ambrocia looks down. When I watch her dance I know she loves moving her body and when I see her with her children I know she loves motherhood. But she doesn't want to have this conversation, she opts for head in the sand.

Emerencia is calculating. I decide she is my entry point. I speak directly to her, but all of them hear me.

"If I were you Emerencia, I would get tested. You are so brave, you were ready to take off for Alaska when I met you, surely you can get tested?"

Now, she looks down and says humbly, "No, Judy. You are wrong, I am too scared to get tested for AIDS, too scared."

Nobody else says anything. I slowly scan the group. It is clear, they understand their peril but are immobilized by fear. They will do what they can to support Anna. I know that, but our conversation is finished, done. I ask Wonder if she will walk to the tuck shop and bring back a neatly wrapped, steaming hot package of fries for everyone to share. All previous ideas of what I would accomplish today have dissolved, and I sit with the girls waiting as they peel back the greasy grey paper and pour ketchup over the fries that already have a glug of vinegar and a liberal dash of salt.

When I reach the co-op the next week my car is filled with cabbages and sardines, e-pap and long life milk. Regina reports that Anna is still very weak but she is sitting up now. She took a taxi for her second check up at Tintswalo hospital on Friday and came home with many pills. It is common practice to have HIV+ patients prove their reliability by showing up for two visits before the precious anti-retrovirals are dispensed. I try to explain to Regina about the T-cell count and anti-retrovirals, but she is confused by this science so I let it go.

"I will go to see her now and take her all the things that David and Neil sent."

This pleases Regina, and I remember when David and Neil came for a first visit to Mapusha last year. The women were thrilled with them, inspired by David's words and health and vigor. After they left Regina said to me, "They have the kindest eyes of any men I have ever seen. " This was high praise, indeed, from Regina. They hold a special place in the hearts of these women, and I hope the rumor that Leslie's group will finance David and Neil's Positive Health workshop in Acornhoek next spring is true. I desperately need their great skill to impress the girls with the need to get tested.

I ask who would like to go to Anna's with me to act as interpreter. Wonder volunteers. She tells me she did the laundry for Anna and Vusi this weekend. She wants to help, and I appreciate her by my side as we walk up the path to the door. She knocks and calls out "Gogo?"

There is no response, so she carefully opens the door. Anna is sitting in a chair and I see with relief that her hair is neatly covered by a bandana today. Last week her hair was uncovered and I was impacted by the naked vulnerability of her sparsely pigtailed scalp. This is much better, and as I start pulling things from my bag she smiles like a small child receiving presents and claps her hands in thanks. I have Wonder explain that sugar is her enemy now and Anna looks embarrassed when Wonder reports that she usually takes five teaspoons of sugar in her tea. I bring out the little saccharin dispensers that Neil has provided, knowing that sugar is probably her sole source of energy at the moment. Sugar feeds her wasting disease, her digestive tract is scarred by the systemic yeast infection so common in the H.I.V.+ reality.

As she fingers my gifts, I consider how to inspire her. I can use David as an example of what is possible, the Great White Hope, but that doesn't seem enough. I search for the phrase, the idea, the inspiration that will continue to nourish her while I am gone.

"Anna, I sent a letter to many, many friends in America about you. I asked them to pray for you and they all wrote to me and said they are praying for you. At my parents' church yesterday your name was read aloud in the service and everyone in the whole church prayed for Anna Mduli."

Wonder translates my words and I watch as Anna's eyes get brighter and brighter and brighter, as though a light has gone on that has never been lit before. She is glowing. I hug her goodbye.

"I will be back by Easter. We will all pray for Anna and I want to see you dancing again when I come back. Remember what David says, 'You can do it!'"

## Home and Home Again

My five-week trip home was filled with Mapusha and I was happy to be returning with all sorts of good news for the women. People were coming on board from many different angles. We were going to have a show next Thanksgiving at an upscale fiber gallery in Seattle. Gail's marimba band played at a fundraiser, and the rugs looked very professional hanging from free-standing wooden frames made by a friend. Rugs sold, orders came in and scholarship money was raised for Syndi to receive business training. It truly seemed as though my women's weaving cooperative was poised for success and I kept mentally pinching myself with the pleasure of it all.

The plane from Johannesburg to Hoedspruit is a 20-seater and flies low, so my single seat by the window let me revel in the vistas below. First the city, showcasing both the leafy heights of the rich suburbs with their sparkling swimming pools as well as the over-flowing townships tinted with the haze of smoke from outdoor fires. Soon this urban scenario dissolves into wide fields of maize still green from late spring rains, and next the dramatic hills begin and transition us from the fields of the highveld to the bush of the lowveld. The visual texture of the bush is incredibly soft with so many, many small leaves on the short, wide trees. These tiny leaves are precisely engineered to catch as much water as possible but the impression created is of an inviting pillow of yummy greens.

On my first ecstatic trip to the bush with Leslie's gang, I surprised myself with a recurrent flash fantasy of jumping off the edge of any of our many viewing spots. I wanted to float towards the inviting soft green cushion of the bush. This persistent imagining seemed to perfectly hold the mood South Africa inspired of wild abandon and total trust. Suddenly I'm eager to get off the plane, impatient with the confinement, longing to be surrounded by the rich, raw reality that is my adopted world. I look forward to this next African chapter which I have a sense will grow my work beyond the mission yard and out into the community. I will be living on an edge as always with life here, clutching for trust as I grope my way forward.

Black dots below must be a herd of wildebeest or buffalo milling about, I watch them with my nose pressed to the window. Leslie is in residence at our home and will meet my plane. We do a strange dance together these days, trying to find a way to remain housemates, though I have stepped out of her teaching realms and my name has been taken off the letterhead of Seeds of Light, the humanitarian branch of her organization of which I was co-founder. We are down with a bump and taxiing on the runway. The Acacia trees flutter and the grasses flatten as we pass. I welcome the hot sun and revel in the huge blue above me as I walk down the thin metal stairway from the plane, so happy to step onto South African soil again.

Leslie stands in the grass by the runway in a crowd of greeters. She looks lovely as always and just seeing her in an elegant straw bush hat and casual, flowing white linens I suddenly see how perfectly she embodies all the qualities I so wished for in my mother. She radiates just that sense of a graceful self-possessed woman that I was so hungry to know. She effortlessly inhabits the arena where Mom was unwilling or unable to go. Leslie was right in line with my fantasies of what a woman should be. My no-nonsense Quaker mother with her sensible shoes and shy reserve was not.

I catalogue this interesting insight as I roll my suitcase towards her. We hug, collect my bags and head off in our jointly owned VW Kombi for our jointly owned home in the bush. I happily fill her in on the fundraisers, the donations, the rug orders and new designs.

In all my back and forth between America and Africa, I never feel fully back until I take the turn into Acornhoek and become a passing part of the bustling scene at the center of town. I smile watching a large woman in a bright dress saunter across the road with a 12-pack of toilet paper balanced on her head. A knock on the roof startles me, and I turn to see Emerencia's dreadlocked head outside the window. She is dressed for town in a tight, shiny dress with a revealing V-neck and her bountiful hair is slightly subdued with a red scrunchy. I lean over to open the door, and she slides in with a smile. She welcomes me home and politely asks after my family. Why is she in Acornhoek, I wonder.

"It is Angy's brother, he is in the hospital," she says, her expression turning serious. Angy has been a close friend since childhood and she probably knows this ailing brother well.

I ask, "Is it AIDS?"

There is a ringing silence in the car and I drive on past the hardware store and the hospital where the pedestrian traffic increases. I wait, hoping she will explain exactly how I offended her. We have talked of HIV, we have talked of testing, we have talked about all of this. She is my most communicative and curious apprentice, so I am puzzled. I know I've offended but I don't understand the offense.

"Judy, do you think every black dies of AIDS?"

Her tone is accusatory and her dark eyes flash. I feel confused for in truth the death of a 28-year-old in the village would almost surely point to the deadly virus and she knows this. But this isn't about logic. I'm hurt by her attack energy, like an insurgent ducking out of the jungle to shoot, and then fading back behind the trees. I am also impressed. Neither her mother nor her aunties nor her fellow apprentices would have the nerve to confront me with such anger, such judgment. I have to bow to this level of courage.

"Emerencia, I'm so sorry if you felt I was disrespecting blacks. It doesn't have anything to do with color for me. I'm just scared of AIDS. I care for Angy. I don't want anyone to have to struggle with the terrible disease." I know she can feel the truth in my words and my posture and her hot outrage cools a bit, her face smoothes.

"It is not HIV. He has been tested." She turns to face forward as we sit still while a herd of black and white cows crosses the road followed by an old man gently flicking a leather strip to move the slow herd along.

I can't help but recall Anna's repeated claims that she had been tested before she had the final test, the test which was positive. I ask how Anna is doing and Emerencia responds that she is fine.

Gladys waves wildly as we pass her fruit stand, and I slow the car and put my hand out the window to touch her hand and receive her greetings and her pleasure that I have returned. Can Emerencia truly think I'm a white racist or is it just her recurrent fear that she is not good enough, that somehow something is lacking in her and everyone knows it? Does she feel AIDS is just another proof that black people are less than whites?

She told me once of a day when she was sent home from grade school for not having the correct school shoes. Her father had recently left her mother and the family had to move from their big concrete house to a small mud house. They were poor. She feared the mud house would melt in the summer rains. In telling this painful tale I saw the wince of remembered pain when the teacher ordered her to leave the classroom. Hot shame is often paraded as hot anger. I know this, but I don't quite know the words and rules of the shame game over here. Mostly, I want to sigh out loud, very loud, for I'm disappointed. Emerencia and I just stepped three giant steps backwards on the trust continuum.

When I pull the car up under my favorite amarula tree and cut the engine Emerencia thanks me, gets out of the car and makes her way into the cooperative just as the older women tumble out the front door to clap and ululu and welcome me home. Anna Mduli is there and I stand for a moment with my hand in hers. She is thin but not skeletal and she looks beautiful to me in her printed brown shirtwaist dress and her trademark red bandana with the sparkly edges. I look into her eyes and there is that glow, that light, mysteriously turned on weeks ago. It is still there, maybe even brighter. She tells me she has her power back and lifts her thin arms to flex her biceps and then begs Regina to explain to me how she is helping others in the village now. She says, "Not afraid," and pounds her chest with her thin fist.

I wish I could tell her the story of the Sunday service at my parents' church where I spoke to the congregation about my work in South Africa. I climbed to the pulpit and began telling her story, the story of how she was affected when she heard that this congregation was praying for her. I tried hard to help them understand how simply being on their Sunday prayer sheet had made her feel special for maybe the first time in her 60 years, American people she didn't even know were praying for her, Anna Mduli. It was a highlight of the trip for me, not only because of the proud hand squeeze Mom gave me when I returned to the pew, but because I felt as though I was able to convey to the congregation the way that they had made the difference in the life of one woman on the other side of the world. Explaining all this is way beyond our communication lines so I say to her, "I am so proud of you Anna. You are on David's team now, no?"

Regina translates with a smile.

Anna nods her head emphatically, "Yes, Anna on David team.".

I marvel at the lion courage of Anna taking on the stigma of AIDS that riddles her village as I watch Emerencia talking quietly to Angy, probably detailing our conversation and my transgression. I shake my head and wonder if I will ever understand the workings of this world and the varied strands of my role within it. How could I know that Anna, who had an abysmal T-cell count of 33 when I left, would rise up as she has, and how could I explain Emerencia's outburst so thick with mistrust?

I gather the women together after lunch and tell them of the orders and gallery shows we have lined up in the coming year. Regina asks me to explain what a gallery show is. I help them to imagine a big room, bigger than their studio, with white walls and shiny wooden floors. On the walls will be the weavings of Mapusha with little signs telling visitors who spun this wool, who wove this piece and how much it costs. I want them to feel my own excitement for this opportunity but I see the worry in Regina's face and the slight confusion in Lindy's eyes.

"What will we weave?" asks Gertrude.

"You will each weave whatever you want. Your weavings will be like the clothes, the outfit you would wear if you could go to the show. Your work will introduce you to the guests who come to see Mapusha." I cross my fingers that this clothing metaphor will catch their imagination. I want them to understand the idea that their tapestries are design statements. I know they understand their clothing as a statement. I have many times watched an elegantly dressed women emerge from a patched tin shack with rocks holding the roof in place. Taking a moment to scan the faces before proceeding, my general sense is that the older women are worried about this show, not sure if they understand how to do it correctly while the younger women are wondering when we will get down to the real purpose of the meeting, their salaries.

Salaries are going to have to be set now that the "Adopt an Apprentice" program has come to an end. For the last six months the cooperative has each month received a sum from the States to pay the eight young women to be trained but now their salaries are the responsibility of the cooperative. To come up with approximately $2,000 a month is going to be a challenge. What is really needed, aside from the magical appearance of some marketing genius volunteer, is help from local people, the nearby lodges, and the wealthy whites who make the lowveld their vacation destination. South Africa, this is where we still have nothing.

Emerencia clears her throat and directs her gaze at me. I understand that she is prodding me on the issue of their salaries and I decide, on the spot, I will turn this one over to Regina. I am not in the mood to be ambushed by the young crowd yet again today. It is decided the girls will earn a monthly wage of $60, which is low but far better than any one of them was earning before they came to the cooperative. They seem generally relieved that they have been considered and will be included in the monthly payroll.

# Blowups at Blyde

As I pull into my usual spot by the lodge I notice that there are some people gathered by the deck chairs where I often sit with Vicki. I make my way quietly past the zebras who are busy munching the grass outside the lapa. It seems the group are all just leaving but I get the sense that there is trouble on the reserve, probably with the staff in their miserable little compound up the road. I have the sense to remain quietly waiting for Vicki to bid them farewell. She will fill me in.

The set of Vicki's eyebrows, slightly raised, alerts me to the seriousness of the situation. Mala, the impala, comes over to nudge at me for pats and I listen to Eugene, the chairman of the homeowners association, tell Vicki he will e-mail Brad tonight. That must mean it has something to do with our lot, but Eugene will only speak with the single male property owner, Brad (Leslie's husband.) I look into Mala's liquid eyes and remember my beloved Leela, a black Labrador Doberman mix.

"It's Able," Vicki tells me with a deep sigh as she sinks into the cushions of the rattan chair. "He is in jail in town. Seems he and Curtis got into a fight last night, he pulled a knife and Curtis is in the hospital. Eugene wants him fired and banned from the reserve. They are going to leave him in jail."

I feel my nerve endings going into high alert. Curtis works for Eugene and Able works on our property.

"But that isn't fair to Able. No one really knows what happened do they? Eugene is being a bully and Able is his target. To leave him in jail is mean, wrong. He is punishing him already."

Vicki's son John has walked over in the interim and he hears what I say and asks incredulously if I truly understand what Able did. He stands above the love seat and stabs an imaginary weapon again and again and again violently into the cushions. I watch him with horror. It isn't not Able's anger but his that I see. I don't know the truth about Able's actions but I am beginning to feel stifled by this place and the sense of being an outsider on many levels is growing, looming larger.

"Leaving him in jail? Firing him without giving him a chance to speak for himself? Is that how all South Africans treat each other?"

Young John backs off, goes to the other side of the patio to smoke a cigarette in silence. Vicki shrugs her shoulders and doubts I will be able to influence Eugene in any way on Able. Night is falling and we sit surrounded by the sounds of the hot, spring night. I imagine the compound on a Friday night. It is a group of small round concrete buildings where the gardeners and maids live. There is a small central yard with a dangling bare light bulb. They cook over little electric burners in their rooms and have a cold water outdoor communal shower where they line up each morning. It was payday yesterday, end of the month so they all had money and there was probably beer and dagga (marijuana) there. The figures are shadowy, but the prickly pride of these men is palpable to me in my imaginary scene.

Who knows what happened, who provoked whom and why? I couldn't pretend to know. In my vision, the pride of the black men in the compound is not different than the pride of the men who recently surrounded this table.

"You know, somehow the Afrikaners and the Africans are so similar, so macho."

Looking at each other and we burst out laughing. I am grateful that she usually understands me even if she doesn't always agree. I am a bigger sap than she is with people, but I watch her with the animals around her and I know her own heart is soft beneath the businesswoman, lodge-hostess and boss. She struggles as I do with the inconsistencies of this new world we have chosen.

We sit quietly together as the stars begin to fill the sky. I will call Eugene myself, and fight for Able, but I am not in the least optimistic that my views will be heard or respected. I stand and give Vicki a hug.

My rondavel glows like a prize in the dark but I make my way into the main house to call Eugene. It feels empty as though echoes are bouncing off me like bat sonar. I move into the little office room with the phone and start to pull the curtains and then decide it is better to look out into the night as I talk, or try to talk, with Eugene. Able is our employee and Eugene has no right to make unilateral decisions on his fate in the name of the board. I sit and dial the number, holding onto the anger that will propel me through the conversation.

"Eugene? This is Judy Miller from plot 56 and I want to talk with you about Able."

He responds with a tirade on Able, and his loud voice holds all sorts of authority, from his job to his chairmanship of the Homeowners Association here at the reserve and, of course, his rightful role as a man speaking to a woman. He is shouting by the conclusion.

"I do have the right to ban him from the reserve and I will. You know nothing of these things. Your opinion means nothing"

I'm getting hot at the arrogance of this man.

"Get him out of jail Eugene." I yell. "That is what Brad would want, I promise you."

He goes on and on, and by the time I hang up I think he will get Able out of jail, but I'm not sure. I don't feel exhilarated by the possible win. Rather, I'm worn out and somehow defeated. I didn't want to fight. I don't want to fight. I hate being surrounded by people who see a whole different world than I do when they look out their window. There is so much fighting that could be done for the others in this country, the black others who live a totally different life than these whites.

Closing up the big house, I'm finally free to walk down the stone path to my own little round home. I never quite open the wooden door without remembering the time when I opened it to see a long dark snake curved along the tiles. But, no black mamba tonight and the bed looks soft and delicious. I turn on the water to run a deep bath and drop in too many drops of lavender oil.

I'm upset about Able in the jail in Hoedspruit. He shouldn't be there with the hardened thugs of the area. I shudder to think of the scene within the bars on this warm Saturday night. I've heard it is tough and violent, and he isn't. Or is he? Try as I might, I cannot read beneath the surface. I miss things, big things, often.

## A New Home

It feels as though I am preparing for another jump. The Able incident coupled with the disappointment of Komogelo's opening solidify my state of separation in the Hoedspruit world. Vicki is a sturdy friend but she is a businesswoman with a husband. It is Nelspruit and the farm of David and Neil that beckons. They, too, are working hard to make things better, and they are way off any beaten path and wildly creative. Heading up to their home in the hills for the weekend makes me smile and I know a plan for change is brewing.

It feels great to be lounging with David and Neil in our own corners of the big L-shaped couch that dominates their living room, ready to begin a marathon watch of "Angels in America." David has the corner of the couch closest to the kitchen, the phone and the front door, while Neil is in the corner where the two couches meet, the spot with the most pillows and the least accessibility. I have the other end, which is worse for watching TV but best for conversation.

David loves to stage events. He has something in the oven that smells rich. Meat and dumplings perhaps? There is the beaded African bowl always filled with candy on the sculpted wooden coffee table and tea has already been served. This is a new HBO series, recently boxed into DVD's, about AIDS in America. It is a tear-jerker, and David knows the play as well as he knew the AIDS world itself while living in the States. He went through the slow death of two lovers and many, many friends. He says we will both need Kleenex, there is a fresh box next to the candy bowl.

Relaxed and warm with these two friends of mine, I let myself drift back over our conversation this afternoon. I told them I wanted to leave Blyde, and its horrible homeowners association, and buy into their farm with the money from the sale of the Blyde property. David is pleased and Neil says he would like to have me on the farm.

They have wrestled this land from the bush in the last six years and planted Baobab seeds, lemon trees, giant ferns and a garden of exotic orchids. They have tried having members of Neil's extended family living in the houses they keep building on the land but nothing has worked out.

"We're ready to create our own family of friends," David declares.

Ramani was their first American to buy in and though she is rarely here, I am enjoying the benefits of her house and phone and car. They have plans for more like-minded folks moving onto the land and it sounds like my long held dream from the early 70's, community living. We settle in to watch the heartbreaking, uplifting movie. David and I pull often from the tissue box.

The next day blossoms into a soft spring morning. On the stoep of Ramani's farm home I stop to swallow the view of the greening valleys and the rounded granite hills. This will be my base. I walk down the concrete steps towards the main house, through the field of mangos where I stop to examine the size and number of pips. The bright scarlet flowers of the winter's bougainvillea are fading on the wall just as the flowering pear opens into full, sweet creamy blossoms. I can hear the buzz of the bees above.

As I thought, Neil is out in his garden, kneeling by a newly planted patch of aloes. It is my favorite way to visit with Neil, to squat by his side with my arms resting on my knees and watch him with his plants. He is carefully patting some white stones around the base of the small succulents he has just planted. I think he knew love with plants way before he knew it with people. His devotion, his practice, his offering is in his garden. He stops his work to light a cigarette and I reach out my hand to take a puff, share this sacred sin with him. I've had my own long love affair with cigarettes, but I fight it and only occasionally allow myself to bum a cigarette and enjoy that hit of harshness to my chest. We stand quietly enjoying the morning and the smoke.

"Will it work for me to live here? Create my own home here?"

Considering, he carefully squeezes the remaining tobacco from his butt and pockets the filter.

"Yes, absolutely, but you will have to stand up to David. No one does, but you really must and you can. You have to be able to fight with him and then let it go and move on."

I consider his words in silence.

A rooster crows in the distance. Neil begins to tell me of his vision for a big vegetable garden at the top of their property. He loves the combination of dreaming and planting, similar to his coupling of science fiction with statistics. He is a researcher at heart. We saunter up the old dirt drive startling a gang of vervet monkeys in the mango trees. They skitter off over the top of the wall into the trees across the road screaming at us or at each other or simply releasing tension as they go. Ramani's house where I stay is on our right and the original homestead farmhouse, now empty rooms for guests, sits at the top of the property. Behind it is the small home they built for their since-retired maid.

Neil stands, feet apart with his hands on his hips and I can feel his delight at the prospect of planning and creating something new, a new challenge, a new project. I watch him as he stares at the untamed grasses and weeds to be converted. We wander around the future garden and suddenly, he stops. "Why don't you renovate Emma's old cottage, get Stephen to help with the design. Create your own house here on the farm?"

Just then we hear David calling. Though I can't see him, I know he has his hands cupped around his mouth and he is slightly irritated that Neil has disappeared.

Neil smiles. "Gotta go. My feeder is calling me to eat." He rubs his hands together delighted with his idea. "It will be perfect"

I go up to explore what looks to be the beginnings of my new home. I agree it will be perfect, a little nest of my own with David and Neil just 100m below me. Climbing the stairs I feel the lift of being up here in Nelspruit on the farm of these deep thinking, fast acting friends of mine rather than down in the valley of Blyde surrounded by the rigid minds of the homeowners.

I have plans for the weavers and it involves all those bulky plastic containers of natural dyes that I lugged over with me from the groovy fiber store in Seattle. I will spend the morning playing with the colors and the skeins of un-dyed wool that are draped on the couch.

By dusk the courtyard is hung with many drying skeins of colored wool. I've used the thick leaves of the aloe to hang the dyed skeins of wool. My favorite is the deep earthy orange of the skeins dyed with natural madder dye. Concrete blocks weight them down so the twisted yarns dry straight and long. They hang in the breeze from a broom handle and I go get my camera to document my delightful day and the site of what is to be my new home.

## Apprentice stew

Daily I go to the studio and laugh with Regina, Gertrude and the three Annas while the apprentices test, challenge, and baffle me. I feel like a blindfolded athlete in our interactions. We are far from a smoothly functioning, cooperative team. When I walk into the studio on Monday morning with the colored skeins looped on a pole, Anna Mduli begins clapping in celebration. The women all gather to see the colors of the plant dyes. Gertrude, the official dye master of the cooperative, carefully removes the cotton string that is wrapped in a figure eight to keep the yarns orderly during the dying process. There is a stripe of un-dyed white where the string was too tight to allow the dye through. Gertrude doesn't say anything but I take the hit with good grace.

"OK, I am not as good a dyer as you are Gertrude." She laughs.

Regina is particularly taken with the shades. She understands the subtle but real difference between these colors and the colors they have formerly made in the iron pot over the fire with the battery acid fixer. She fingers the purple yarns and nods her head. "Yes, these are very beautiful. I will like weaving these colors together."

I suggest that with these colors she create her own abstract design. She has an artist's sensibility with colors. I watch her as she weaves and I know how she loses herself in the flow of colors. It is the same way I used to melt into the colors as I wove. I look forward to seeing what she will create.

As I turn from the table with the wools, I catch sight of Ambrocia as she is tying on her stampi, the shapeless cloth covering to protect her clothes. Before the stampi is in place I see her belly. It is round. Not fat, round. She sees me looking at her and smiles shyly, lowering her eyes. She is pregnant. I go over and congratulate her but I feel slightly queasy.

I silently muse. Ambrocia is having unprotected sex. What about the others? My gaze goes around the room to the other apprentices at their looms. Angy has been looking particularly lush lately, could she be pregnant as well? And Syndi, she was off last weekend in Pietersburg getting registered for her courses. Where did she sleep up there?

Ambrocia giggles at my pretend words with the baby, "Are you going to be a girl? Are you going to be a weaver like your Mama and your Gogo?"

She isn't sure when the baby will be born but she thinks around the new year. So she is six months pregnant. It isn't surprising that no one told me but I feel a pang of sadness at my outsider status. I'm used to being the trusted confidante. In America people tell me their secrets, but not here, not in the studio, not with the apprentices. Standing by Angy's loom I ask about her weekend. She turns her big eyes to me, slanted ovals that always remind me of Egyptian eyes, and says, "I am pregnant, too."

"Oh Angy, you must be happy. And the father? Is he a good man?"

She answers, "Yes, a good man." She tells me her baby, too, is due at Christmas time.

Angy was the one apprentice who dared to tell me when I first met her that she dreamed of having a husband and a family one day. I wonder if the father of this baby is really the one of her dreams. I want to be happy for these two young women, but it worries me. Sitting by Regina I ask how she feels about the new babies.

"Babies are always good. We will love them at Mapusha and it will be like the old days when all the weavers had a baby on their back. Emerencia, Kamoocho, Syndi and Ambrocia all grew at Mapusha."

"Yes, but I worry about AIDS. I didn't know any of the young women had boyfriends."

Regina chuckles, "We will just have to trust in the Good Lord."

The apprentices decided that on payday Mapusha would have a special chicken lunch for all the women of the coop. Today is the day. Ambrocia and Angy calmly slit the necks of four scrawny white chickens. We made a special trip to town yesterday to buy them from a road stand with a slew of scrawny chickens squashed into small wire cages.

Wonder chose the four that we wanted and they huddled in a cardboard box in the back of my car on the way to the coop. I was a little horrified when they were still scratching around in front of the studio this morning when I pulled in. Now, the cooks are draining the blood from the chickens into an enamel bowl and I wonder with a squeamish shudder what they do with that bowl full of chicken blood. The other young women sit on benches under the shade of the dye shed waiting to begin plucking the white feathers from the limp forms. The fire is already sending flames around the base of the cast iron pot and Angy rises to salt the boiling water.

I decide to join them and see what I can tease out this morning. Kamoocho has gained weight over the holidays and I tell her she isn't working hard enough. I say she must have spent too much time sitting on her butt. She can't help laughing at my talk, laughing until her whole body shakes with silent mirth. It seems there is something more under the surface; her laughter is bigger than my words. I let it go.

They are almost ready to put the chickens into the pot so I leave them to their work. Walking around the building I realize Emerencia is behind me. When I turn she asks if we can talk, "in private." She's ambitious, so this might be a new scheme to move her forward. Or it could be a problem with her sister apprentices, or with her mother or her daughter or her brothers. I don't know, but I'm curious and vaguely honored. She carefully closes the door to the studio and turns to face me saying,

"Judy, I have a problem."

I go on high alert. Is Emerencia actually going to tell me something private and use me as a counselor of sorts? I smile at her and tell her I would be happy to help if I can. I close the door carefully and put myself into my counselor mode.

Afterwards, I linger in the quiet of the storeroom and silently applaud this young woman, her bravery, and her high emotional intelligence. She has instinctively done the only thing there is to do with her fear. She has owned it, spoken it, and shared it. I learned long ago that one can't heal a problem hidden within you alone in a closet. I do know how hard it is to open the door, let someone see. After all these months with the apprentices, it is Emerencia whose walls came down first.

I go out to sit by Gertrude as she knots the fringe on a bright African Landscape rug she has just taken off the loom. This is our most popular rug, variations on the first rug we made joining the orange, browns, blues and greens of Africa, letting them flow one into another in curves and waves up the length of the warp. I ask if she is happy with the weaving of the apprentices.

"Yes, I am happy. The girls are working hard and Mapusha is gaining power again."

She nods proudly, full of optimism and good humor and I feel that slight frisson of fear as I get a glimpse of the big ways I am involved in the renaissance of this weaving cooperative. I sit down with my lunch plate on my lap a little away from the gaggle of apprentices. I don't bother them about speaking English with me today. Let them speak their familiar Tsonga. I pick at my chicken and pap as I watch the eight young women eating together. Syndi throws her head back with wide laughter and the others join in.

My little taste of time with Emerencia in the storeroom reminded me of my job as a counselor in Portland. Then, I felt as though I knew what I was doing, and I knew how to do what I was doing and, honestly, thought I did it pretty well. Here, I can say that I never know what I am doing, never know how to do it, and any sense of competence eludes me completely. The apprentices have baffled me and I am flying by the seat of my pants on a level that I could never have even imagined. And then, to top it all off, these women, each of them, is becoming increasingly dear to me.

I think I helped Emerencia but still a vague fear of responsibility shadows me, like distant heat lightening. I make myself a toasted cheese sandwich, the easiest thing possible, as I consider if my fear comes from the responsibility of finding money for their salaries each month. Deeper down, I know how little of their lives I really know. What Emerencia's confession yesterday revealed was how much I care about her and Sampiwe, Regina and Gertrude, while they remain, in many ways, strangers to me.

When I go to the co-op I ask Emerencia to come into the storeroom. She is quiet and serious and tells me she does feel better after our talk.

I am pleased, relieved. I decide to tell her a tale of my own.

"Want to hear a story about my school days?," I ask to break the tension and she brightens slightly and nods. "I was in the 6th grade, so probably about 12. My right breast was beginning to get bigger before the left one, which upset me." Emerencia smiles and I think I may have found the right way to meet her. "Mostly, I just cared about how I looked so when I saw an ad on TV promising beautiful skin with Noxzema, I decided to try it." She again nods her dreads with understanding, for the women here are always smoothing cream onto their own hands and their babies. She understands this beauty ritual. "There was a big jar of it in my mother's medicine cabinet and I smeared it on my face and then my arms and legs. When my father dropped us off at the playground I walked down the steps feeling particularly good."

I have her attention fully as I mime feeling good. "Just as I reached the bottom step the older girl next to me yells out 'Smelly, Smelly!' and starts pointing at me. Soon I was surrounded by a circle of girls chanting 'smelly, smelly, smelly.' I tried to run at them but they backed off as if I were infected or poisonous."

"What did you do?" she asks. She's wide open with my story.

"I just walked off the playground into the school building as though I didn't care."

"Did you care?"

"Yes, I did care, very much. I felt lonely and sad." It's the right answer. Tears fill her eyes and I nod my head, remembering the sensation of being an outcast.

She holds my eyes as she humbly thanks me and I watch her go back to her loom. I feel a glimmer of hope. Maybe caring is enough to help these young women, I tell myself with a small bubbly sense of hope. Somehow the young women here need encouragement to take a step. They need to be emboldened to find the courage to stretch their wings. But, the real question in my new hands-on-in-the-world position is can I create a context for these young women to venture more and more out of their protective shells? I don't know. I can try.

## 89th birthday celebration

The Bambi road is a mountainous stretch beginning in the lush lowveld of Nelspruit and traveling around and up steep inclines until suddenly it emerges into the wide fields and long vistas of the high-veld. I began driving this morning amid golden-leafed trees and red tinted dry grasses but now as I get closer to Johannesburg, the winter palette has taken over with its pale yellows, greens, grays and browns.

Mom is coming to visit for a week. We made these plans for her trip when I was last home and I organized a raft of friends to help my sister. Dad has a full schedule of caregivers and she is on the plane now, planning to spend her 89th birthday with the women of Mapusha.

It will be interesting for me to have so much time alone with her. Last time she was here I was sick and we were staying with friends. This time it will just be the two of us driving back down from Johannesburg tomorrow, staying with her friends Anne and Stuart, and then down to meet Mapusha followed by two nights in a private game reserve. I consider and decide this really is the most time I have ever spent alone with my mother. Maybe this will be my chance to get to know her differently, without Dad at her side.

Maybe our conversations will have more depth, more honest vulnerability than usual. We really never have talked much. I interrogate most people in my life, but I've always spared her. She's very private.

I try to imagine delving beneath the acceptable framework of politics, family and the day-to-day order of things with Mom as I would with a client or friend. It feels almost like a violation with her.

Driving has always been a zone in which I can let my mind play and dream, suppose and consider. Now the road, bordered by bright pink cosmos, is long and straight with wide fields of dried corn stalks stretching off into the distance. I begin to circle around the questions of women and shame, me, Mom, Emerencia, Regina. I want to better understand that instinct to hide, to protect and cosset secrets. I have never known what lives within the walls of my mother's privacy zone. It's like a steel plate both shutting things in and shutting things out. I have wondered for years what she is scared of revealing or losing, and I wonder now if it doesn't center on that 'less than' premise which I am picking up so often. I consider wryly the translation of the Tibetan word for woman; a lesser incarnation.

I feel into my own belly to see if I can find a clue with resonance. Is it somehow linked to that shamed female I confronted in the mirror when I saw myself bald naked? Is it some Eve-based shame passed down through women generation after generation the world over, or is it more particular? I remember at thirteen stuffing my blood-streaked underpants into a fluffy pajama bag doll rather than go talk to Mom. It was the Irish maid who found them and assisted me with the strange ritual of belts and pads. Mom couldn't breach her own barriers to assist and instruct her daughters. Really, I don't think she ever knew the crafts of being a woman that I so yearned to learn. How could she teach what she didn't know?

Letting my mind soften, I find myself drifting back into the warm, tiled indoor swimming pool at Baldwin, the private girls' school I attended through sixth grade. Dressed in the school issued, shapeless, thin, cotton bathing suits, my sixth grade class stands together awaiting permission to go change back into our school uniforms when, surprisingly, our gym teacher asks for a volunteer.

She wants one of us to show her the latest dance craze, the twist. I eagerly raise my hand and she chooses me to demonstrate. We have all practiced the twist and the mashed-potatoes in the locker room, but this is public and it feels very risky. I do my best to swing my hips just as I've seen the teenagers do it on TV. I twist from side to side with my bare arms crooked at my sides and my fingers snapping. I look up to Miss Wells to gauge her response and she's looking at me in a strange way, a hungry way, a way, I know, is not right. I stop my twist, suddenly awkward and step back into the circle of classmates feeling as though I did something wrong. Her response to my dancing was definitely wrong.

The shame of that moment of exposure still burns in my memory and it has the same taste as the shame I saw in my eyes on the day my hair fell out. It was as though by that pool long ago, I had been seen and what I was was not good, not right. It's as if I swallowed the two entwined together, being seen and being bad. It wasn't something I could ask Mom about, though she probably had her own stories of being seen and being wrong. If I knew her stories would it change mine?

The signs directing drivers to Boxberg and Pretoria are beginning to multiply and the traffic is increasing. I need to stop my roaming in the past and focus on the road ahead.

She is the last to emerge through the doors of the customs hall and I am greatly relieved to see her blunt-cut, bright, white hair at the end of the line. She's wearing sturdy sneakers and a fleece for the cold, and looks stooped, and weary as she comes through the big silver doors.

She perks up immediately when she sees me. I hug her, welcome her, and then bustle about taking her bag and getting us on the correct elevator to the parking garage where my car sits. It is actually Ramani's little pick up truck, bakkie, I'm driving but she gamely climbs up into the utilitarian passenger seat and fiddles around to snap herself in. Walking back to my side at the wheel, I see that she is happy for me to be the leader on this trip. I've never seen her give up the reins of control so completely. Probably, she is bone-tired from taking care of Dad, but maybe she always knew I would be a better leader, maybe she has just been waiting fifty years for me to accept the job.

We settle into the little B&B where I have reserved a room and I urge her to lie down. Since she wouldn't 'waste' the money to either travel business class or rest in London for the night, she has traveled twenty-four hours straight. I know how the trip makes me feel, so I'm firm. She relents, "but just for 1/2 hour, I don't want to miss anything and it is best to get onto a new time quickly." That's right, I chuckle remembering how my stoic, schedule-bound parents always just move into the new time zone no matter where they are or how large the time gap. On their first day in China, Egypt or France they don't miss breakfast, and turn off the light at ten pm on the dot.

While she rests I fiddle about in the small kitchen emptying the bag of supplies, placing the coffee and filters on the counter with the peanuts, bread, dried mango and slipping the milk, Woolworth's boxed butternut soup and wine into the mini refrigerator. Meals won't be fancy or multi-dish but I don't think she will care. She will at last get to experience being a missionary in Africa, or at least a Judy-style missionary.

I hear the alarm go off and she soon comes into the sitting room and goes to the window to enjoy the sun and the flowers, Birds of Paradise in splashy silhouette against the white of the building.

"I don't know what it is about this country that makes me feel so happy," she says with a smile on her tired face. I hand her a glass of wine and a bowl of peanuts and settle in for our week together, sure that I will learn something to help me find the thread that will untangle the mysteries that puzzle me.

We spend many companionable hours driving together. We visit with this friend and the other and she sees my new home under construction at the farm, visits our friend Sophie on her farm overflowing with AIDS orphaned children. We mostly talk about what surrounds us in the moment and somehow that is as it should be.

When we arrive at the Mapusha studio the women pour out of the door eager to greet my mother properly. Each woman shakes her hand and I am struck by the warmth and respect they pay her. They aren't shy or reticent with her as they are with most guests. She is an honored visitor, partly because she is my mother, but, also because she is an elder. Elders deserve and receive respect in their culture.

She speaks with each of the women, asking Gertrude about her grandchildren and admiring the way Lindy is weaving a tapestry of many colors. She holds Sampiwe on her lap and goes with Wonder to the storeroom to choose something special for Sally. It is a treat for me to watch her with them, to see her be the center of their full-hearted embrace. She isn't shy, but almost childlike in her pleasure at being with the women in the studio. We've brought a cake and they sing Happy Birthday to her, surround her for a picture in which everyone has big smiles. Mom looks so little and white, the Mapusha women an earthy, dark halo around her.

Regina walks over to the mission to ask the fathers for the key so she can show Mom the inside of their church. I go with the two of them into the simple interior and stand at the back. Regina curtsies as she enters the pew, Mom bows her head. They both kneel on the hard wooden kneelers and I'm struck by the two of them, their strength, and their similarities despite living such different lives. Regina was abandoned by her husband and had a very tough time raising five children alone in the Apartheid world of separation, whereas Mom lost her father and her security at sixteen when The Depression hit. She lost her first baby at three days and her beloved brother too young, but she has had great security in her marriage to Dad. I'm deeply moved seeing the two of them, kneeling together in the dim church.

We need to leave the coop to get to the private game lodge and reluctantly we head towards the door. But, no, no the women insist we must first hear the song the apprentices have made for Mom, they have been practicing.

It is Kamoocho who takes the lead in their song. She belts it out, "Where have you been hiding her all these years?" This is the refrain, asking Mom where she has been hiding me. Mom claps her hands at the conclusion. The young women are pleased with their performance and I am touched. They joined forces to welcome my mother and signaled their appreciation, and their thanks to me. We shake hands all around and everyone follows and waves and smiles as we drive away.

Mom is tired, dozing as I drive through Acornhoek. Glancing over at her sleeping with her mouth slightly open and her head dropped forward, I feel a new level of tenderness for her plucky, indomitable spirit and I wonder if I can't just let go of my focus on the walls and the secrets.

She thoroughly enjoys the private lodge and the game drives. She is happy to finally see the Blyde Canyon and meet David, Neil, Winks and Vicki, but nothing tops her day with the women of Mapusha. We didn't talk deeply about anything. I tried once when the open jeep broke down on our game drive and we had the great luxury of sitting alone in the gloaming while a new vehicle was found.

"Do you remember when I announced to you and Dad that I was a pantheist?" I ask as we sit, surrounded by the very kind of world that could make me declare my pantheist allegiance again and again.

"Nope, doesn't ring a bell." she answers.

I don't know where I even learned the word, but being here I now remember climbing a tree at Ashbridge Park and deciding from my perch that I was a pantheist.

Looking at the stark shape of the nearby leadwood tree, I continue, "I felt something more of God sitting up on that tree branch than I ever did in the Church of the Redeemer."

She looks slightly uncomfortable and I let it go. I wish I knew if she felt the same sense of connection to some unnamed greater reality as I do. I remember long ago being in the garden with her. Something about the way the sky and the zinnias and the sunshine merged made me suddenly know what it was to be a part of a web larger than my parents, my family, and my neighborhood. It was invisible but alive throughout my small being and has been ever since, always. I don't know and I won't know what her god looks like, what her greater reality feels like and how it moves and works within her. But then, why should I?

We sat on in silence until the replacement vehicle arrived, and then continued our drive. We followed a male leopard marking his territory, a four-legged master athlete moving soundlessly through the bush, undisturbed by our presence. He lifts his leg to warn others away and we follow slowly, mesmerized until his path moves down into a gulch where we can't follow. Then, we just drive in the dark through Africa's rich world with the soft winds of the bush in our faces, passing through the sudden bright smell of a flowering something. An occasional call of the night birds punctuates the silence. Neither of us speaks.

At the end of the week when we arrive back at the Johannesburg airport Mom is officially sick, a flu which has her weak and unable to eat. This will not stop her from leaving. No, she feels she must get back to Dad. I get her a wheelchair at the airport and with a heavy heart try once again to convince her to stay, or at least promise to rent a room during her eight-hour layover in London.

"Poof, I'll be fine," she says weakly from the wheelchair. I kiss her good-bye and she thanks me again for our trip. "I loved every minute and I'm so proud of thee."

Tears roll down my cheeks when an attendant wheels her out where I cannot go. I'll have to warn Steve, my brother in New Jersey, of the condition in which I am sending our mother to him. Suddenly feeling both lonely and absurdly free, I head out of the airport and back to the car. I'm really glad she came to see my world and satisfied that I did my very best to make her trip special. I understand her more completely now, but more from what was not said than what was said. I know we all have secrets, both secrets from the world and secrets from ourselves, but I don't think Mom knows much about what she hides or why. She simply isn't interested. I'm the one obsessed with understanding the why and how and what of others and myself.

Our time together did give me something. It was just being in the world with her and seeing her genuine kindness and the respect she gives to everyone. I wasn't ever much interested in her political actions, but spending a week with her I understand as I never have before that she is a naturally shy person. It was in the arena of politics and social action in which she burst through her own barriers. She hated the Vietnam War and marched for peace. She fought for women to have the right to be Episcopalian ministers. She championed Bishop Tutu, and worked to get the Philadelphia banks out of South Africa during Apartheid. These feats never meant much to me, but watching her talk with Wonder and Ambrosia, the staff at the lodge and the gardeners at the farm, meant a great deal.

As I begin the dip down through the mountains towards home, I let myself dream about how I can move the women of my small Rooiboklaagte world forwards. Being with Mom reinforced my sense that the best thing I can do to heal my fears, her fears, the fears of the women and girls I see daily, is not about understanding old wounds but, instead, encouraging small acts of courage now, now. Breaking barriers, taking the next small step forward looks different on my white haired, sensibly-shoed, ever polite Mother than it does on my own spiked hair, orange Crocs, more vulnerable, volatile being. Yet, no matter who or where, I know the central push must be to meet the fear and move through it.

I remember Mom and Regina kneeling together, side-by-side in the church and feel respect for how these two who were born without the ability to vote have moved it forwards. They did. I can. By the time I reach the lowveld I know that the best way for me to move forward is to do all I can, more than I have so far, to empower the women of Rooiboklaagte. Maybe I will encourage Emerencia to challenge me, maybe even inspire the older women to challenge a man. I want to find ways to help them to smash through their own self-created boundaries and barriers, and I will.

# Part Three

GROWING THE CIRCLE

# Helpless at the Hospital

I have big plans for the day, but when I arrive at the studio on the New Year's opening day Regina is missing from her post at the loom closest to the door. The bench is empty, and when I look towards Gertrude, she is looking at me and shaking her head. Regina is at the hospital, she explains, and shakes her head some more. Emerencia fills me in, reporting that her mother was coughing and she had no strength, so she went to the hospital this morning in a taxi. I am surprised that she is here, and not with her mother, but she assures me that Kush, her younger brother, went with Regina to Tintswalo Hospital.

I have never been to this hospital but I remember too well the public hospitals I visited in Johannesburg where birds swooped from the rafters of the large dormitory style rooms, and where only some of the sick children had their gogo by their side. Nurses were in very short supply. I shiver to consider Regina at the mercy of this deeply overburdened public center, and I suggest to Gertrude that maybe I should go see if she needs anything.

It is decided I will go and so I leave everyone to their work and set off, glad to have a task to consume some of the nervous energy that is running through me. Wonder runs out the door waving for me to stop. My water bottle is in her hand and I stop, slow and force myself to breathe deeply. Now is not the time to be witless, now is the time to use Regina herself as my model and move with a centered quiet, steadily forward, step by necessary step. I thank Wonder for her care and drive down the dirt road. There is a strange silence on the road as all the children have started back to school today, with their new uniforms neatly pressed and their hair specially braided or shaved clear down. September was always an exciting month for me—a new grade, a new teacher, a new pencil case and binder. This is their September, they are returning from their longest holiday, the summer holiday, for a new school year in January, but I miss their laughter and antics as I drive slowly down the road. There is little to distract me from worrying about Regina.

I turn off the Acornhoek road where the sign points to the hospital. Along the backside of the parking lot are stands with piles of bananas, sweets and single cigarettes for sale. Someone is cooking chicken in a big iron pot over a fire. Many people, mostly women, are walking towards the gates of the hospital.

Hospitals give me the willies. I am about as bad with physical ailments and pain as I am good with emotional, spiritual and mental tangles. I am squeamish around anything that involves blood, and I cringe in the face of physical suffering. When I had to enter the private hospital for my lumpectomy I somehow called forth some old warrior-being heretofore buried in my depths. She made jokes, moved fast and acted tough. I made it through the initial operation on this adrenalin surge, but when my temperature rose and I had to return to the hospital two days after being released, I had a complete meltdown. Tears ran down my face when my oncologist came into the emergency room where I lay on a gurney and told me I had to be checked back into ward C to receive intravenous antibiotics. I felt I had somehow failed and was going back to prison and I just didn't have the strength to keep up the brave front. The warrior evaporated.

Another red flag around all things to do with a hospital came from my ten hospital days with a bone infection, osteomyelitis, when I was two. My parents abandoned me to a crib in a room with many other cribs. I can still envision the head of the toddler across the way. The walls were painted pink and the linoleum tiles on the floor were grey with pink. My mother came daily and threw a wrapped package into the crib when she left, but it didn't make up for the fact that she left me there alone again and again.

All this jitters through me as I become part of the throng going through the metal stiles into the compound. There is no one bothering to check people in or out and everyone seems to know where they are going. As I come through and look around at the covered walkways to various buildings, I feel a tap on my shoulder and turn to see Donald's mother, Clara. I know her from the reserve where she cleans house for Marius, but seeing her here with her good clothes and elaborate turban is disorienting. Suddenly I understand, she is here and she is happy because Donald's wife must have had her baby. I pretend to hold a baby in my arms and she nods and points to the furthest building down the walkway. I return the nod and tell her I will come but first I must find Regina.

There is little option for me other than to wander and look around for clues. I am the only white in sight and these folks aren't ones who would speak English easily. They all have a purpose and I don't want to bother them, so I scan the long lines of people waiting to get through the door of this building or that. It is obvious that one building is for children. Everyone in the line is either carrying or walking with a young child. I see a hugely pregnant woman walking with a friend at her side to the building Clara had indicated, so I have obstetrics and gynecology nailed down. But where would a woman with a bad heart go? I am searching for an answer when I see her. Regina is standing in a line in the heat of the midday sun. I go over to her. She is literally grey.

"Oh Regina, shouldn't you be in the shade or sitting down as you wait for the doctor?"

She greets me cordially as I have so often seen her greet her many friends and acquaintances in the bank or on the streets of Acornhoek. Ever polite, she asks how I am today and I ask why she has to stand in a line if she is sick. She says simply that this is the line to check into the hospital and it is slow today, she has been in line since she got here 3 hours ago.

And where is Kush? I'm upset by the situation and wishing I had brought Gertrude or Wonder or Emerencia. It can't be right that she has to stand in line when her heart is bad, she is weak, it is hot and she hates the heat. I frown at the impossibility of it all and know I am beaten. She won't fight to bend the rules, and I can't fight for her. It might work for me to fight with whites or to fight in the bank or with the traffic cops, but I can't fight here. If I went blazing up to the front of the line it would embarrass Regina. My way isn't the way it is here, and she knows it and I know it, and so I say simply, I will be back.

I look over my shoulder to see her with feet planted hip distance apart for balance, her elbows bent holding her handbag and her head slightly bowed. She is probably praying. I proceed towards the building of birth and babies. Along the concrete path I see a man on crutches with one empty pant leg neatly pinned closed, a very old wizened woman in a wheelchair, a baby with a bandaged head and on and on—so many too thin people, so many empty eyes.

It isn't hard to find Gloria with her new baby girl bundled in her arms in a dorm room full of mothers with their new babies. The small black Sister is taking her blood pressure and Clara is busy with something I can't quite see. Gloria is proud of her new baby and speaks to the nurse in a rapid sequence of Tsonga that I understand is about me. I smile, for I know she is saying that I chose the name for the baby. Donald was working with Able on our property and came to me for a loan when his pregnant wife was sick. My gift earned me the right to name the child. I had suggested Grace but when I used the image of a graceful athlete in trying to translate the word, Donald settled on Graceful. I'm glad the baby is a girl.

The nurse explains to me that it is the grandmother's job to bring a red, braided, wrist band for the child and to prepare a muti-bag with special expensive ingredients purchased from the local sangoma to protect the baby from evil spirits. This is what Clara is preparing. Muti, magic, spells and curses are the way of things here, and I watch Clara finger her bits in a bowl and mutter words that only the ancestors are meant to hear and understand.

Baby Graceful is tired out from her journey into the world and rests peacefully in her mother's arms. Donald, the father, will not see the baby for three days, and then it will be weeks before anyone other than grannies can see the child, the nurse tells me as she bustles about, righting the sheets and pillow. I guess I have made it to granny status, an honored visitor to an, as yet, unprotected child.

I wish the little muti-bag that Clara prepares could be hung on Regina's wrist. I lean in to look more closely at the baby tucked in the center of that bundle of pink blanket and she opens her still milky eyes. Tears slide down my cheeks for the joy of a new being and for Regina who is at the other end of life. And I shed more tears for all the beings in lines at this hospital and in hospitals everywhere, and tears for myself as a two-year-old abandoned in a crib years ago, and on and on. These tears of compassion christen brand new baby Graceful.

When I go back, Regina has passed through the line and Kush is leaning against a concrete post.

"She is in. Her heart is not good," he says.

His handsome young face frowns at the state of things and I offer him a lift back to Rooibok. As we settle into the car it occurs to me that when her heart problems first began would be good information to have. Kush is friendly. I notice his hands, he has the same long-fingered hands as his mother.

"When did your mother first have heart problems, high blood?"

"It began when my father returned sick to his sister's house."

"Just before he died?"

Kush nods. We drive down the main street of Acornhoek and I put the pieces together in my head. It makes sense. The anger and shame arguing within Regina's being as she was once more forced by her culture into the role of wife to the man who deserted her. I can feel the indignity of her public humiliation, and again, of course, the helplessness. My blood pressure would probably rise, too.

At the co-op, Kush waits outside as I give the women the news of their friend. Everyone comes out and Kush solemnly tells them Regina will stay in the hospital until they have the right pills to keep her heart right. Anna Mbetsi leads a prayer circle for her, and everyone files calmly back to their looms. They are so used to the hospital, sick people, unforeseen this, that and every other thing.

I visit her in the hospital the next day where she calmly sits in a bed with a scarf tied neatly around her head. She tells me what she wants most is a drink of milk. I go and buy her milk. That problem, at least, is one I can solve.

## Syndi's Grand Desertion

Regina does get the right pills, and I bring her more fresh milk and homemade salt-free vegetable soup. On her first day back she walks around the studio, stopping to greet each woman to praise their work and thank them for their support. It is what my mother would do.

I am happy to be again sitting by her side as she weaves, but today I am also a little distracted because Syndi has not arrived and we have a group of tourists coming soon. Syndi unfailingly charms our visitors and thrives on the attention so I don't understand why she isn't here. I turn from the window to focus on Regina's work, which has taken a whole new turn now that we have the natural dyes. It was just last week I handed her a palette of dyed skeins. I recognized her glad response when she first saw the array of colors. It was subtle but I knew the look in her eyes as she slid her hand slowly over the yarn. I, too, sometimes just fall into a color. I want to devour its beauty, merge and become it or have it become me. Her new weaving is an intricate blending of these colors creating a beautiful flow of soft purples dissolving into deep, sea blues and greens. It is fluid and organic, and I shake my head with wonder at the sophisticated artist who lives within.

"It is very beautiful, Regina. It reminds me of a flowing river."

She agrees, and I wonder idly as I glance out the window hoping to see Syndi coming up the path, if Regina Hlabane has ever in her 59 years had the time to sit beside a flowing body of water and gaze at the dancing patterns of movement and light. Maybe it's not water she is remembering with this blend of colors. Could she explain to me why she weaves as she weaves? Could I explain to her why I wove in a similar flowing style when I sat cross-legged in front of my own frame loom? Maybe what she pictures is what she experiences within herself, the internal flow of energies. That would be something that no one could take from her. I remember sitting day after day in a month-long silent meditation retreat. I wasn't weaving colors together, but I watched the ebbs and flows of internal energies in all the colors of the rainbow.

Syndi strolls into the studio looking exceptionally, strikingly, suspiciously dressed up and beautiful. Remaining slightly hidden on the bench by Regina, I watch as she carefully takes a seat in the chair near the door, the chair usually used by guests. She smoothes down her immaculate white skirt and pats her newly permed hair. Some mixture of chemicals has created a mass of shining ringlets which frame her pretty young face. All is perfectly set off by the pale yellow of her ruffled blouse. But the thing that really catches my eye is her shoes, high heels. I know something is up with the shoes. The women of Mapusha love their shoes but there are only two times when I have seen them pull out the heels - church and travel. They dress all-out for God and they dress all-out when they are leaving the familiar territory of their village. Why does Syndi have heels on?

The other apprentices look too absorbed in their work. They probably know what Syndi is up to and know, as well, that I don't. I turn to Regina and ask her if she knows why Syndi is so dressed up?

"Her mother told me she is going to Pietersburg today."

"Why?"

I am shocked, but Regina doesn't appear to know the reason for this trip of Syndi's and I start to panic. She knows we have a tour today. I will get to the bottom of this only by going over to speak with Syndi. Reluctantly, I leave my spot by the loom and Syndi notes my approach. She smiles and stands to greet me. She is keeping to traditional manners though nothing feels normal about this moment to me.

I nod my head and leave her the space to fill me in, but I can feel the tension of a potential fight begin to harden my diaphragm.

"I am leaving Mapusha, Judy. I am going to live in Pietersburg."

"Today? You are going today? For good, not coming back to Mapusha?" I'm both shocked and not shocked. "What about your contract with the women? What about the tour today? Surely you won't leave before the tourists come?" I am hot all through and I know my face is red by now, and I know every woman in the room is listening to our exchange.

"Yes, I have to leave today, now. I just came to tell you good bye."

"But why didn't you talk to me? Why not tell me what you were planning to do yesterday, last week?"

She shrugs, still smiling, not a smidgen of guilt. I look around for support to her mother, her sister. But no one is going to involve themselves with this. I realize with a start that somehow this problem is mine and mine alone. I am outraged. Don't they feel it? She is letting the co-op down in a big way, and she tells me as if she is telling me the day's weather. She is not filled with remorse. She is at once casual and proud, defiant and happy.

"The taxi will be here soon." She walks towards the door and calls out something to the women in Tsonga as she lifts her hand in a gay wave of farewell.

I don't raise my hand to play the "farewell, travel well" game as the other women do. I feel completely ambushed by this saucy young girl and I feel impelled to run after her and beg her to come back, to just please do this tour group today.

I follow her out the door but turn right, while she heads for the road and the taxi that will carry her off to a new life. I walk around the studio to the empty dye shed and look for a bug-free place to sit down and try to collect myself before the guests arrive. It will fall to me to carry out Syndi's role of gracious greeter and guide, I suppose, glumly. I don't want to be the star of the cooperative, the voice. I want them to be the stars.

I sit on the small circle of crumbling concrete at the base of the shed's corner pole. Looking out over the fields of the village to the mountains in the distance, I feel the upset in my heart. She acted as though she was happy to be gone. My anger slowly deflates and my mental inquiry starts to swing from Syndi to myself.

What did I do wrong? I can hear her eager voice telling visitors about her dream to help her mother's cooperative rise up and be strong. She sounded like the savior of Mapusha. But, really, wasn't *I* the one wanting to be the savior of Syndi and Mapusha? Or maybe I thought I needed Syndi to assist me in saving Mapusha. If my intentions are so selfless and noble why do I feel so betrayed and humiliated?

Gertrude steps out of the tumbledown outhouse and hesitates a moment before she comes over to where I am sitting in my funk.

"Gertrude, wasn't it unfair the way Syndi walked out on Mapusha?" I ask truly wondering if this behavior is fine with the older women of the co-op.

"It is better this way, you will see. Syndi is Syndi. She is not a weaver."

I know what she means, and I nod my head and try to swallow the fact that I am the only one who feels hurt and angry. And now, the older women are worried about me, not about Syndi.

I smile and tell her "Okay, I believe you. I will stop being mad at her. I promise."

She nods and I watch her walk around the building, her steady gait soothes me.

There is a gang of boys playing soccer on the field across the way. They are running up and down the field in haphazard shorts and ragged tee-shirts with bare feet in 100-degree heat, and suddenly I get it. Syndi is a player, just like these kids on the field. The village is too small for her. She had to leave as Paul warned me long ago. He said the winners would find a way out. Syndi did. I knew she would, but I wanted it not to be so. I will recover myself but the cooperative has taken a hit with her departure.

It makes me pause when I consider how many, many other misunderstandings brew in the pot of Mapusha and me. Our relationship is not a simple one. I seem to float around somewhere between boss and friend. And the friend relationship is weighed down by the immense differences between our lives and cultures.

I stand and brush my seat as the bus of tourists comes bumping down the road towards our driveway. We will rally. Who knows how this morning's incident will reverberate through the studio and through me. Maybe, just as I didn't see Syndi's imminent desertion, I don't see how this will change things for the better. Maybe she shone just a little too bright and there will be a greater sense of community with her gone. As I round the corner I see that Emerencia has come out onto the steps to greet our guests.

Emerencia does a great job as a tour leader. She is articulate and funny, a bit less of a wow than Syndi but stronger on truth. Her relationship with the other members of Mapusha is more honest, clean, clear and equal. As I knew from the start, Emerencia isn't a weaver, crafts woman or artist. She is a people person, and this just might be a perfect niche for her. It makes great sense to pull in the tourists from all the surrounding lodges and to do that we need someone to speak to them who is not white and not American. She is perfect and I am pleased at how things have smoothed themselves out. My eternal optimism now rests on Emerencia and her potential to play a key role in the whole.

## Rag Rugs?

The Joburg interior designer's snitty comments still ring in my head, such that when I get a lead on free fabric for the co-op, I jump on it. I've always loved rag rugs, their homey texture and complex colorings. In my studio in Boston years ago, I wove rag rugs with linen strips. And now I am hoping this fabric bonanza will give the apprentices a new product. Somewhat funky rag rugs might be a product more in line with Joburg's high-end design, a little edgier than the neat, woven wool tapestries. It is a challenge to have salaries for fourteen women each month.

I study the slip of paper Heidi gave me with directions to Sparky's Car Repair. It is in the way outback of Hoedspruit. I weather a challenging maze of turns and mis-turns but arrive at last. Three big dogs lie on the greasy concrete workspace and a jumble of broken cars languish among the high weeds of the yard. I count several black men in overalls and one big white man in shorts and high socks, Luan. Stepping out of the car, relieved that the dogs barely lift their heads, I call out to him, and he replies cheerily, greeting me in Afrikaans.

"Moira. Missus. Heidi's friend?"

"Yes, Judy." I reach out my hand to shake his and look into pale eyes beneath bushy eyebrows and a shock of greying hair. He has a friendly face and his big hand grasps mine warmly.

"Ach yes, come, come this way."

Behind the garage there are more sprawled dogs and a metal door with a rusty padlock. As he searches his massive key chain, he asks me about the weavers, the 'aunties' he calls them.

The door finally gives way with a puff of dust all round the edges and I peek into the space. It is dark and there are spider webs, dark stains on the wall and a faint odor of animal something or other. I compare my flimsy flip-flops to Luan's sturdy leather boots and gingerly step forward into the room. I reach the nearest of the big bulky burlap bags and untie the crude fastening. White fabric, yards and yards of it, are squashed inside. Wow! This is a find. If it is actually cotton the dying and design potential is unlimited.

"Oh Luan, you would actually let the women have this fabric free of charge?"

I am touched. Just when I had given up all hope of help from the Hoedspruit community this giant of a mechanic somehow offers a gift that could really help the cooperative.

Luan nods his head and begins a tale about his missus who collected the fabric. I don't really understand how it all came about or why it sits here now but he seems truly happy for me to take it. He needs the room for car supplies and if I don't take the fabric he will burn it. I'm just a little disappointed that this isn't as much about helping the women of Mapusha as about reclaiming his space but still, it will help the salaries. Too often I wake in the middle of the night and play with figures in my head, making sure we have enough in the bank account, calculating the next month, and this order or that. Despite all the help I receive from Portland and my friends in the States, it is a struggle. If we could weave a stylish product without the cost of the wool and the spinning it would be great.

I thank Luan profusely, and he calls his workers to heft the bulky bags and squeeze as many as possible into the back of my car. I'm a little ashamed of how pleased I am that it is not me who has to go further into the room and disturb whatever lurks amongst the dingy bags. Sometimes the macho attitude here falls to my advantage. I shake Luan's hand again, give the men who carry the bags a generous tip, and drive out of the yard very pleased with myself and my loot.

When I arrive with my carload at the cooperative the next day I am looking forward to telling the women about Luan's gift. But when I do, they seem skeptical. I try to explain my vision of rough, rag rugs and my hope that this will be a line for the apprentices to take up. I try to rally the younger women to come out to the car with me to get the bags of fabric while the older women arrange a place in the back corner of the studio for the new supplies to be stored. Ambrocia is the first to pull one of the big bulky bags out of the back seat and the others gather around to see what's inside. Unfortunately, when the bag is opened the white fabric is dotted with dark bat turds. When Ambrocia guardedly pulls the fabric out we all see the yellowish urine stains here and there as well. Emerencia turns up her nose.

"And you think rich white people will want to buy rugs made of this?"

"I do, Emerencia. When we wash and dye and cut the fabric into strips it will make wonderful cotton rugs. Can you see it Lizbeth?"

Lizbeth has such a good sense of design, she must see the potential here. But she, too, is fingering the discolored, white fabric with a certain disdain.

"I do not think it will be nice to cut this fabric." She is sensitive to the fibers of wool that float about as she weaves and is anticipating the fibers of this process will be worse.

"Hey you guys, I'm trying to find a way for you to earn your salaries. Don't you see you can weave without the cost of wool and the cost of spinning? The weaving will be fast with these strips of fabric and we can dye it and make wonderful stripes and geometrics. These rugs will be more modern than the wool rugs, just as you're more modern than your mothers."

Wonder and Ambrocia and Angy buck up a bit with my words and dutifully begin to lift the heavy bags to their heads to carry them into the studio. I watch slim Angy heft the bulk to her head and then turn my attention to the other four.

"Have you ever heard the expression about the glass of water that has only some water in it?"

They shake their heads, looking utterly bewildered.

"In America we have an expression about that glass of water. Is it half full or half empty?"

They look at me with furrowed brows and silence.

"It could be called either half full or half empty. The faithful person, the hopeful person will call the glass half full. She knows that more water will come to fill the glass. The one who has no hope for the future will call it half empty. That one is just waiting for the time when there is no water at all to put in the glass."

Emerencia understands what I am saying and begins to explain to the others in Tsonga. Water is a precious commodity here. Slowly, one by one they begin to get it, and they laugh when they understand what I am trying to say.

She says, " You are like the Fathers. You are telling us to have faith in God when we look at this ugly fabric. To imagine that these bags hold all the money we will earn from our rag rugs."

"Yep, you got it! We need to practice thinking half full."

Now the older women are inspecting the fabric and Lindy has raised her eyebrows which isn't a good sign.

"What do you think?" I ask her.

She explains, in as few words as possible, that she doesn't think this fabric will dye well. It is treated with something that will . . . She trails off lightly, shaking her head.

Regina and Gertrude look concerned but, as always with these two, they are willing. I explain again my plan for this free fabric, and my rationale.

"We will try," says Regina stoically.

Gertrude is ready to get out the big iron pot, start a fire and boil some of the fabric.

"We will clean it," she says, ever pragmatic. Clearly the real offense here is that the fabric is soiled.

I agree with Gertrude that we should try dyeing some of the fabric at the same time that we boil it clean. We begin the process of collecting wood and water. The older women go to the mission to fill plastic containers with water to bring to the dye shed where I sit on a bench. I know that they all came out to help, and to show the younger women their solidarity with my new idea and me. Appreciation washes over me as one by one they empty their containers into the big pot. We all clap when Anna Mduli walks around the corner with the heavy water container on her head, proof that she truly has her power back.

The apprentices are slowly, cautiously pulling the fabric out of one of the bags. They look as though they are being forced to handle cooties, but I hear no snippy sneers. They are at least willing to give my wild scheme a try.

The dyeing commences. Gertrude is stirring the cloth in the pot and it looks as though Lindy is right, the dye is only tinting the white fabric. Emerencia and Angy are pulling the fabric from the bag and soaking it in the tub before it goes into the dye pot. Wonder and Lizbeth are wringing out the dyed fabric and hanging it to dry on the metal rods. It is all going smoothly. The pale colors have a certain beauty to them. I imagine bathroom rugs with stripes of pale blue on the palest of pink background.

A slight discomfort runs through my veins though. This is really the first time I have forced my will on the group. How can I lead them without controlling them? That is what I want, but I don't seem to be able to finesse the right balance. I am in a strange position. I say I am not the boss. It is their co-op, but here I am being the boss, making the decisions. I want the girls to really step-up and take responsibility for their salaries, but at the same time I refuse to let them fail. I cannot bear it when there is no money in the account at the end of the month. To even consider that any of the women's sixty dependents would suffer because there is no money this month drives me to distraction. I don't take a penny in salary, so it isn't hard to understand the gratitude of the older women, but the younger women are puzzling. Added to the mix is the fact that the cash from selling my house is diminishing and I will have to do something soon about supporting myself.

"Ohhhhh, nice purple." Lizbeth cocks her head and seems to agree that the shade of the latest batch is good.

"Just keep making different colors Gertrude. I know the dye does not take well, but we can make good rugs with these light colors. Make every color, like Jacob's cloak."

Gertrude doubles over with laughter when she recognizes my words as from her own Bible stories. I laugh with her and feel a surge of gratitude. She's always so ready to work and so ready to laugh. Things are moving along fine.

In the storeroom I look at the books to see what is to be done about salaries and supplies this month. I fasten my mind on the rag rugs and imagine them taking off, with orders coming in from all the posh spots in the country, Mapusha women finally gaining recognition in their own country.

## My Wonderful Tree House, and A Dog?

I am happily lying on my bed in my new bedroom, a loft at the top of ship-galley stairs in my new home on David and Neil's farm. My new home was designed by Stephen who knows me well. A simple renovation of a small unused building became a nest with wings when he added a loft. I smile each time I click the garage door open, park my car and walk down the stone path to the covered porch. I've planted jasmine bushes along the path and have started a slightly whacky semi-circle of raised beds for lettuce and herbs. The whimsically curved path from the porch leads down to David and Neil's house, 72 steps below, and having my own secret entrance makes me feel a part of their tribe.

A small bowl of cat crunchies and an open window have succeeded in luring up the very shy cat, Gus. He now lies at the foot of the bed, untouchable still, but he is my companion to welcome in 2006. Relaxing back onto my pillows I enjoy the airy feeling of this space and consider where Mapusha is after three years.

The cooperative is creeping forwards. We have a website. We had a show of our work in Seattle, and emails are going back and forth between Sarah in England and me about Mapusha's possible entry into an international trade show in Birmingham next year. This would mean a multi-rug commission for the weavers. Slowly, slowly we are beginning to attract tourist groups to come out to the studio and see the crafters at work. Emerencia is stepping forward in her role as tour guide and I have given her the task of doing the accounting for the cooperative in the new year, which is a weight off my shoulders.

We've learned much since our first attempt at serving lunch to tourists. Vicki came with a friend and Shirley Ann, the woman who first introduced me to Mapusha. We sat on benches back under the small tin roof of the dye shed. The younger women served chicken from a pot that included feet and necks, and every few minutes various women went past on their way to the outhouse just behind our luncheon. Vicki's friend blanched when handed her plate, she saw a chicken's grisly toenails. Vicki and I still laugh about it.

I have changed my center of gravity from Hoedspruit to this new home on the farm in Nelspruit, two hours southwest, where I will spend long weekends. I'm still trying to find the right place to spend nights during the week while I work with the co-op. In the New Year I will try out Wit's Rural for three nights a week. It is a small community not far from Acornhoek where an open-minded couple I know live. I still have one foot in the Blyde reserve through my friendship with Vicki.

I smile at the small circles of blue glass in the wall of my bedroom. I gave the builders only one instruction as to how to place them. "Not symmetrical." This instruction threw them completely, how does one do 'not symmetrical' correctly? Really, you could boil my whole clash with a certain mindset down to those who can do asymmetrical as well as symmetrical. The fourth set of windows, over the loft balcony, opens onto blue sky during the day and star-drenched dark at night.

I worry about Mom and Dad and the burden their increasing frailty puts on Sal's shoulders. It's a lot for her to deal with her family, teach full time, and cross the street nightly to sit with my parents and catch up on their day. I will go home to give them all a good shot of support in June, and receive my own shot of support from the increasingly large group who want to do what they can to help my Rooibok world. I tick off the many ways people have stepped forward to assist: a new roof, running water, a sink, rug commissions and visits to the co-op. The creche has locks on the doors and some toys for the children. Increasingly I feel the pull to do more for the community, more to feed the children and to empower the women. My attention should be on marketing for Mapusha, and that is always my intention, but then something happens — a house falls down or a child has no food, or a pregnant mother has no shoes, and it goes on and on.

I turn out the light and put my head on the pillow, happy that Gus is still with me. Here we go with new year number four with the women of Mapusha. Tomorrow I will try out Wit's Rural and see if it feels right for my weekday nights.

The light is dusky as I drive up the muddy road to what the signs call Wit's Rural Community Public Accommodation. Low branches drag on the roof and I see busy dung beetles in the mud on the side of the road. This is where I have chosen to stay for three nights a week now that I am free of the reserve, and am no longer a homeowner. Leslie, Brad and I amicably agreed on a price for my share of our home and I realized they were happy to have me go, as though I were a cuckoos' nestling who no longer fit in their sparrow's nest.

Wit's Rural is deep in the bush, but just on the other side of Acornhoek. I will be closer to the weavers here, and can do yoga on Thursday evenings with others from the community. I will be in the bush, paying a very small nightly fee, and I will at last be a part of a community of folks trying to help the same sort of people I'm trying to help.

After driving for twenty-five minutes on the narrowing dirt track I have not seen a single car, a single person, or even a light. At the gate, way back at the beginning of this trek, the friendly man told me in halting English that no one would be at the center this late. He had the key to my place and pointed me in the right direction with a hand signal that meant just keep going. True, there aren't many choices. Slowing, I inch forward with all my senses on high alert. I do love the bush, but now at the witching hour I feel like a foreign body in a very big and somewhat threatening place.

Around the bend is an open area with a cluster of small round buildings. There is movement beside one of the huts and my heart leaps happily for a moment. A dog, a big friendly dog. But no, the neck of this animal is too big and humped for any breed of dog. I stop the car and hold my breath. The form on the lawn is a hyena, a big one. My heart thumps away. I watch the animal who ignores me as he continues to chew whatever it is that drew him here. I check the locks, roll up the window and cut the engine. The number on the site where he stands is #4 and the heavy wooden block attached to my key reads, '#5 Impala Cottage'.

Watching him chew reminds me of the bear I once saw way up in the Wallawa mountains of eastern Oregon with Joe. It was a long northwest summer evening and we had backpacked up to camp by the clear mountain lake. It was dusk when we saw him across the lake. His stance was eerily human. I can still visualize his standing form in sharp detail. But back then I had a lake between us, and Joe beside me, so it was more thrilling than scary.

This hyena will head off into the bush at some point I'm sure. I've never heard of hyenas attacking humans or cars, but what of the lions and leopards. They are the ones who leave pickings for the hyena, and as far as I can tell I am the only human anywhere near this bared patch of bush. It isn't the hyena that gets me as much as being in the middle of the animal free-for-all zone.

The night birds begin to call as the dusk deepens and I sit on in the car. It is strangely peaceful in my little bubble of metal and glass, but I am scared to open the door and venture out to fumble with the key in the lock while fearing something just outside my line of sight. I shiver and reach down to move the seat back so I can hug my knees. At the sound the hyena raises his head. His eyes are yellow. He looks directly at me.

His head bobs down again. I'm not as interesting to him as his bones, which is good but not good enough for me to attempt a race to the hut. The bush and the sky and the grass are all the same non-color for this moment before the bush goes dark and the sky becomes the source of light. The moon is a tiny crescent and the stars begin to show themselves, one, two. I close my eyes and make a wish.

"Courage."

I have taught whole workshops on courage but I wouldn't want my students to see me now. I don't feel brave or courageous. Mostly I wish I could curl into a ball with an ever-so-soft blanket over me, go to sleep and wake up to a beautiful morning with no hyena in sight.

I open my eyes. He is gone. I look again and there is nothing breaking the smooth line of the grass. I feel somehow tricked. I dropped my vigilance for one moment and he dissolved into the night, in which direction I do not know.

Can I do it? Not easily, not without fear, but I hold my flashlight in one hand and the key in the other. I take a moment to banish the whiner from my mind, open the door loudly and run towards the door of the hut. Thankfully the key doesn't stick and the door releases me into the room. I close the door and sit on the bed, breathing deeply.

"Kowabunga!"

I made it and the bare walls and old-fashioned bedspread of the simple hut look utterly luxurious to me. Though the bathtub is old and stained I turn the hot faucet on full force as I, bravely, venture out once more to get my bag and my book from the car. This solitary scenario of woman meets beast in the bush was far from what I had imagined Wit's Rural to be. The central imagined point was being a part of an open-minded community and instead, I feel utterly alone.

## House Tumbles Down

I'm scrambling to find a way to lure some of the many tourists who pass through Hoedspruit out to the studio. And I'm considering what needs to be done and what hasn't been done as I drive to and from the studio daily.

The rag rug production has begun. Lizbeth always wears a mask across her nose now, and Emerencia still often wears the tiniest of sneers at the whole process. Brushing worries aside I appreciate the soft autumn day, and just as I turn into the mission drive, Lindy, Ambrocia and baby Elena come across the field. They walk together from their nearby homes every day with Elena on her young mother's strong back. The grass is still green and I let the beautiful day ripple through me as they approach. Lindy has a peach-colored blouse and I recognize the beautiful silk scarf she has neatly wound round her head, only my French friend Denise would have given such a scarf away. I am sure it was Lindy who made the skirt Ambrocia wears, a flouncing four-gourd pattern made from a fabric rich with red and orange roses. All I can see of Elena is a small peaked pink cap rising from the terrycloth towel that holds her in place. I greet the three of them and begin a new version of my many one-way conversations with Elena. These conversations are always said in a very particular voice reserved for babies, dogs and cats.

"And how are you today missy? Did you let your mommy sleep last night? Would you like to learn some English today?"

Ambrocia chuckles and Lindy smiles. Elena's long curling black lashes begin to rise and her round brown eyes open wide when I bend close to speak with her. Her pretty little mouth that reminds me of her mother's curls into a smile. Ambrosia loves her new baby girl and is a wonderful, relaxed young mother.

We walk into the studio together, still laughing. Gertrude is working on the wall loom to the left of the door, so without thought I go over to her

"Absheni Gertrude, conjohnny?"

She turns from her weaving to face me and shaking her head heavily says, "I am not well Judy."

She isn't smiling which is very unusual and her eyes are full of sadness. I brace myself for the bad news whatever it is. Never before have I been answered in this manner by any one of the women.

"Today when I was walking to work I heard a loud bang." She claps her hand and stomps one foot on the floor to help me understand the sound she heard.

"The house fell down. My house fell down on Sinthe." A single tear trickles down her worn brown cheek.

My eyes fill with tears of sympathy and horror. How can things go so badly so quickly? I express my sympathy and ask how Sinthe is doing.

She is so very helpless. Susan may be her adopted mama but I know Gertrude feels the weight of responsibility for her orphaned special-needs grandchild. I scan my mind for a picture of the house that fell down. I was surprised when on one of my many visits to the Mbetsi family plot, I learned that Gertrude and her husband didn't live in the big house but in a small crooked shed off to the side of the plot. The tin roof is held in place with rocks and probably lacks strong beams of support. I'm sure it was hastily, cheaply built as the extended family grew and grew, as children unable to find work returned home and as grandchildren kept coming. Sinthe sleeps with her grandparents, and the strong winds of this morning must have unsettled something in the shaky structure. Bricks fell, and Sinthe was on the floor. No one was in the room with her and so no one knows exactly what happened. Susan is with her at the hospital now.

"I will help you, Gertrude. We will help. I'll write Gary and Jane and Bobby and tell them that their friend Gertrude needs their help. We will make a roof that can't fall down."

I reach into my purse to find my cell and give it to her.

"Call Susan. Maybe she has seen a doctor and we can know how Sinthe is."

I go over to see what I can learn from Sinthe's aunt, Wonder. Thankfully, it doesn't sound as though any bones were broken and there were no cuts or gashes. Maybe her unresponsive muscles that never behave correctly were somehow helpful in this situation. Maybe something is terribly wrong inside and no one knows what hurts since Sinthe can't speak.

As we wait for word from Susan, I ask Ambrocia if I can hold the sleeping Elena. She nods and standing, bends forward to loosen and let fall the toweling so I can lift the small sleeping body from her back. Elena is warm and doesn't seem to mind that she is now held on a different body. Her small hand slips inside my shirt and rests softly on my breast. I feel her body get heavy with relaxation as she sinks back into deep sleep. I rock her. I rock myself and look around the room at these women who are so accustomed to dealing with tragedy and helplessness. I feel Elena's soft breath on my neck and clasp her gently a little closer.

Sitting with this baby, I am reminded of my own odyssey with wanting a baby. It started in my college years with dreams, vivid dreams of giving birth or of being hugely pregnant and fearful that I would give birth to a puppy. It continued as a fierce longing, and one night I remember actually telling a group of college friends that if I didn't have an appropriate father soon I might just go for a sperm donor.

This sounded exotic and revolutionary in 1970, but my desire was strong and without reason. It was when I joined with Joe that we finally got serious about making a baby, but it didn't happen. Each month I would get hopeful and more hopeful and then crushed when my belly cramped and again and again, not pregnant. We tried temperature taking and endless sex, an operation to clear the scar tissue from my tubes, and pills, but all to no avail. It was one of the many emotional roller coasters that filled my married years with Joe.

When he left to live on a boat in Guatemala, I just simply and quietly let go of the whole package — husband, children, and normal family life. I had already expended all the emotion available for that track. It was time to move on.

I dove into the world of seeking, and learned to grow my heart in other ways. I look down at Elena. I can feel her heart in sync with mine, her breath throwing out tiny energetic tendrils binding us together. Another child to adore, yes, this Rooibok world of mine is stretching and growing my heart.

We wait and wait. Sitting, waiting, I mentally plot and plan ways in which I can impact and help this situation. I write an email in my mind asking for contributions, help for Gertrude's family. I will take Sinthe and Gertrude to the white doctor in Hoedspruit and see what he has to say about her condition. I will do this, I will do that, and I will fix this hole and patch that problem neatly up.

Elena has opened her eyes and is regarding me seriously. Wonder comes to tell me that she talked with Susan and the nursing sister thinks Sinthe may be alright. Disaster has been averted. I return Elena to her mother and ask if Gertrude would like me to give her a ride to either the hospital or her home. I'm exhausted from the feelings and the waiting and she must be more so but she says no, she will weave. Susan will take care of Sinthe.

## Moving forwards, Tiyiselani

Sinthe and Susan and then Regina all combine to start me off on a whole new tangent of community work. One day I am casually watching Regina weave and considering how well-supported Mapusha has been. Money poured in to assist Gertrude with her housing problem, and Stephen helped with Denise's gift to create a sink with running water for the studio. I am beginning to understand how much people like to be of assistance, and when the project has a name and a face and a specific problem many respond quickly, generously. I am getting it. As a megaphone for the problems and needs of one village I am gaining steam and confidence.

"Regina, if there was more help for your community from America, what do you think would be the best way to help?"

She considers my question carefully as she weaves and I sit quietly appreciating her art and her thoughtfulness.

"It is the unemployed women that need help, and the children. They need help with education. That is what I would say. There are too many women with no money and nothing to do, no way to feed their children. They live on the small government stipend for the children and it is not enough. They suffer. And the children, if they do not get a good education how can they find work?" She nods her head satisfied as I consider her well-reasoned response.

"Do you think I should ask Susan Mbetsi to gather the women who are interested? I don't know what they want or what we could do, but it would have to start with a meeting wouldn't it? Maybe Mapusha could be the umbrella for this organization, sort of the mother of this new group."

Regina turns her head slightly and raises an eyebrow, "Maybe."

I think I catch a note of caution there and am reminded that I am as blind when it comes to intergenerational relations in the women's world here. Possibly that is what her eyebrow raise hints at, some sort of etiquette between women of which I am unaware. I thank Regina for her ideas and prepare to set off for a talk with Gertrude.

As if on cue, Susan Mbetsi walks through the door with Sinthe on her back. Sinthe's long thin legs dangle and Susan is out of breath from carrying her here. I greet Susan and Sinthe begins her own special greeting. Gertrude climbs down from the bench where she is weaving a bright African landscape runner. She takes Sinthe and holds her high in the air before placing her carefully on a blanket on the floor by her loom.

I ask if I can speak with both of them. Susan is on her way to tutor a new Father at the mission in Tsonga but says she can sit for a bit. I see she is intrigued. Gertrude sits down on the bench with Sinthe.

"Do you think it would be a good idea to start a club for unemployed women? I don't know what we could do but Regina thinks that this is where help is needed in the village. What do you think?"

Gertrude solemnly nods her head as though she sits at a shiny boardroom table. In her view it is simple, the unemployed women need help. Many people need help, but the unemployed women are young and strong and they have children to feed.

Susan is bursting with ideas and ambitions. Before I know it she has offered to gather a group of women to meet with me to see what can be done to make them stronger. She is delighted with the idea until I suggest that the women of Mapusha, so skilled at running a cooperative, might be the mother organization. At this, her head pulls slightly back and it is apparent that she has objections. I lean in hoping to learn something here.

"What is wrong with that idea, Susan?"

She looks me in the eye and says, "It is better that one group is separate from another."

"But why?" I won't let her off the hook here.

Her mother sits there, not speaking, and looking down at her feet in a posture of non-engagement I have come to know well. She doesn't want to be involved in this conversation. She is being diplomatic. Susan doesn't really answer my question but goes back to the idea of gathering a group to meet with me. I back down, and it is agreed we will meet on Sunday after church, under the tree.


They have chosen my favorite tree as the gathering place for the women and it feels a good omen to me. The tree is old and the trunk divides low so the branches spread out wide over the dusty scrub of the empty veldt. I have loved it since the first time I walked by and saw it alive with skinny black legs and arms encircling its broad, friendly branches. Today, enjoying the welcome shade, I idly watch a small gang of raggedy boys playing some sort of betting game, tossing small rocks with a few grimy pennies to be won. They are too absorbed to talk to me, so their banter fades into the background noise along with the single goat bleating from his station by the sand pile. This is where the snack sellers wait for the children to spill out of the old elementary school. The women sit patiently in the hot midday sun, often lounging in their empty wheelbarrows with their hats pulled low over their brows and their little bags of corn chips, boiled peanuts and single sweets spread out neatly on the ground.

Emerencia tells me that Sampiwe, now in kindergarten, daily begs and begs for a penny to get a sweet at lunch. Pennies, everything is in pennies in this world of so many people so close to the edge.

Susan was at church this morning and told me many of the unemployed women from the community would be at the tree today at 1:00 PM, after church and before the Sunday meal, but she tends towards exaggeration. I am excited at the idea that they will come, and equally fearful that they won't. I lean against the worn grey tree trunk and wish it could tell me of this land long ago when it didn't stand alone, the only tree in a schoolyard. Ants crawl across my foot and I stay as still as possible, hoping they will simply continue on their way.

Susan spreads her worn stampi and sits down on the ground by my side. She tells me her idea that the group have a dual purpose -- to help the poorest of the poor children in the community and to help the women themselves learn skills and find ways to make money. One by one the women appear, approaching the tree from different directions across the dusty fields of scrub. Emma is the first to arrive, tall and statuesque, she bows slightly as Susan introduces us.

"She doesn't speak English," Susan explains, "because she comes from Mozambique, but she is a hard worker. She goes to the river bed to dig clay and makes bricks, herself. Her husband is sick and she has many children."

Susan tells me the story of the women, and they are hard stories. Each of the twelve women sitting in our circle is responsible for more than one child. Only Emma has a husband and he is sick, too sick they say. I tell them that I have friends who want to help them to gain skills so they may find a way to make money. I ask Susan to ask them for ideas, what they think would help them.

As Susan speaks I look more closely at the women in the circle. The little one has gumption. It is obvious from the way she did her headscarf up into a high turban, and the way she watches me, unafraid of eye contact. She is from Mozambique and has two small girls. Her house is the size of a garden tool shed in the States and I don't know what she lives on. I doubt she has the necessary papers to get the $25-a-month child grant that most of the poor women receive. Lena is a Mbetsi, a cousin of Gertrude's clan. She dresses with care, everything neat and well pressed. Susan is still talking with them and they seem suddenly more animated. I listen closely and try to understand what is causing the ripple of enthusiasm.

Susan turns to me.

"We are talking about the poor children of the village, the ones who don't have what they need. How we can help these children?"

They have so quickly moved away from their own needs. I am touched that these women who have so little want to help those who have even less. I think quickly.

"Maybe the first thing to do would be find out exactly how many children are in great need, make a list of them and their ages."

This idea seems to go over well and it is decided that Lena and Emma will do the village survey.

"What about a garden at the grade school?"

This is Susan's idea and it is a good one. Gardening is something these women know well, an area where they feel confident and powerful. We craft a plan to ask the local grade school if we can fence and hoe their back field. The women will do the gardening work, and the produce will go both to the school and to themselves for consumption or sale. Of course there is the problem of water, but we gloss over that issue.

They must go. It is clear their homes and children are calling, but we stand together in a circle while Lena prays for our new venture. They sing a round of 'Amen' and then, again set off across the fields. Susan must go to feed Sinthe, but she takes time to thank me and I can tell by her bright eyes and big smile that she is happy with the way the meeting went.

"We must find a name for our group," I tell her as she lifts her stampi and shakes off the debris before tying it back around her waist.

"Maybe Tiyiselani - we shall walk through all obstacles until we succeed."

I wave to her and sit alone beneath the tree once again. I consider the word. The image of Gertrude walking up the road is what I envision. She continues on, always she moves forwards towards her goal despite the obstacles. There are always so many obstacles here but I watch the women who just keep moving forward.

'Tiyiselani.' I like it.

## Acornhoek meets David and Neil

It is a wondrous co-mingling of my worlds when Seeds of Light hires David and Neil to come do a five-day Postive Health training in Acornhoek. This is their signature book, training and all-around forum for which they are known throughout South Africa, in fact, known over all of Africa.

I am bursting with pride over everything about this happening and have been at a high pitch all week. We drive form the farm each day with David at the wheel, speeding first through the eucalyptus forests of White River, then the acres of banana fields, and finally the friendly townships. Each morning all the women of Mapusha and Tiyiselani pile out of Anna Mbetsi's son's battered white bakkie. We join the bustle and jostle of women. Some are young women in stylish track suits, some older and more rural in conservative dress with children or grandchildren strapped to their backs. In the entrance hall everyone gets an orange and a cup of tea before the day's teaching begins.

It has been a treat to watch my friends doing what they do with such ease and expertise. They communicate effortlessly with these folks. The audience has been disarmed and captivated by their honesty, their knowledge and their unconventional ways. The bush telegraph has been active in Acornhoek each night, so that each successive day has seen a larger group. More chairs are always needed for the opening prayers. Yesterday the count was 350, and who knows how many sit surrounding me in anticipatory silence today.

"Now I want everyone to close their eyes and listen," David announces from his stand in front of the large group. It is the last day of the training and he radiates a new level of seriousness. I would guess we are about to experience the grand climax of the workshop. He has a strong performer streak in him, and a great sense of timing. The moment is ripe for some special something for the group to take home with them. Emerencia, their official translator, repeats his instructions in Tsonga, and there is a sudden hush, a palpable tingle of curiosity in the jam-packed, standing-room-only auditorium.

David begins the guided meditation, his voice taking on theatrical tones as he asks them to imagine they are walking towards a church, their church. He has the total attention of the room and I watch the deep concentration on the face of the granny sitting beside me.

"You are going to a funeral and you greet the many friends and family who are coming to the church as well." He pauses, giving them the time to greet their friends, see their church. A small spontaneous smile forms on the faces around me and I am touched by the trust they exhibit towards David, his voice and this process. I stretch my head to see my Rooibok friends and note that they, too, look to be deeply immersed in this experience David is creating.

"You approach the coffin to pay your respects and you look into the coffin, and it is you in the coffin." A deeper silence fills the room and smiles slowly fade.

"You see your friend coming up to the coffin and you hear her say, "Why didn't you take care of yourself? I need your support. I am very sad that you let yourself get sick and die."

He isn't even using music at this point and the silence is only broken by the whimper of a small baby nearby. Her mother quietly leaves the room and David continues,

"Now it is your mother who comes to say good bye. She is very sad and she says to you, 'Why didn't you care for yourself? Why have you left me to care for your children, I am too old. I need you."

Now the music comes, softly at first, but it touches my heart and my eyes fill with tears though I'm not even truly participating.

"And finally it is your child looking down at you. Your child who is now an orphan, and she says, 'Mama, why did you leave me. I need you.'"

The music continues. After a bit David gently brings everyone back to the room, and as they open their eyes he asks them to stay in silence as we break for twenty minutes. I am moved by the meditation and eager to see how it has touched the others. Gertrude is part of the stream making its way up the crowded central aisle. Her eyes are full and bright and when she sees me she simply touches the palm of her right hand to her heart. She need say nothing more. I stand to join the stream of quiet people moving towards the door.

David and Neil are having a cigarette around back away from the crowds. I go over and hug David. There are others waiting for a word with the star so I stand in the back with Neil. I am glowing. This is the kind of group process that made me a process junkie for years. Everyone has dropped their habitual defenses and they are taking in something bright and new, something more expansive.

Emerencia comes over and I ask how she is doing. I am proud of this, my most thorny of students whose will and prickles have brought her far from the young woman who wanted to head for the Alaskan fishing boats.

"I am doing well," she says with big eyes and a wide-open face. "When David said that about your child and I saw my baby Sampiwe in front of me, I said to myself. Emmy, you must go be tested. You must do it for your child."

I don't know what to say so I just hug her and tell her how happy that makes me.

He did it!

"Do you think the others will agree to testing?" I ask nearly out of my skin with excitement.

"I think so," she says nodding slowly. "I will talk to them."

On Monday, Gertrude solemnly tells me that all of the older women are prepared to take the test to determine their HIV status.
"We are not the ones who should be scared, but we will do it."

I agree and we both look towards the corner table where the younger women are seated. Emerencia is not here, and when I bring up the subject of getting tested with the younger women only Angy comes forward.

"I will be tested," she says with a brave smile. She is a trooper, and though she couldn't weigh one hundred pounds the weight of her family rests squarely on her shoulders. Her father is nearly blind and she has a one-year-old child.

I sit on the bench next to Wonder and speak with her quietly. "What about your child, Claudia? Don't you owe it to Claudia to get tested as David showed you last week?"

She looks straight into my eyes and says "Yes," and her gaze returns to her lap. "But, I am too scared."

Ambrocia won't look up and neither will Emma. Lizbeth looks me straight in the eye and says, "No." I turn and feel the frustration that these younger women can rouse in me. They are so stubborn.

"Would anyone like to go visit Love Life with me to see about testing?"

No one wants to go with me to the bright purple building just outside central Acornhoek. I pass it daily and it never looks like much is going on there despite the purple painted attempt to look like a cool place for young people to go. Emerencia told me that when this government-sponsored health agency opened the young people from the outlying rural communities liked to attend their functions at first. But the parents began to realize that their children were getting into more trouble with these trips to the more urbane Acornhoek central than they did at home in their villages so the Love Life outings stopped.

Inside the small bright Love Life building, green plastic chairs sit in a small empty circle on the dark swirls of the concrete floor. My Croc's squeak with each step and I feel like an intruder in the empty space. I stand at the window and wait. At last a woman in a red dress and high heels appears. She seems surprised to see me. Whether it is because I am a white, middle-aged woman or because few people appear at her window, I don't know. She has a fancy, braided hairdo of extensions and we greet each other. I begin to ask about their services and tell her about the women in Rooibok who are ready.

"We do on-site visits to small business now. We will come with tents and counselors and everything needed."

We are both pleased, and I ask if she was here when David stormed in last week. She chuckles, "He is something, that one."

I tell her how it all came about. One of the young women had the nerve to question his HIV status since he looked so good and healthy. His response was to challenge anyone who doubted his status to walk over to Love Life with him. He will get tested as will any challengers. He walked down the road with twelve young followers beside him.

She gets sober when she tells me that they have been busy since the workshop, sixty people have been tested. Last month, for the whole month, only twelve people came to be tested. It is wonderful feedback for David and Neil. We make arrangements for the team to show up at Mapusha the next morning, and I leave pleased with everything.

Sitting in the car with my cell at my ear, calling Emerencia, I view the strange purple building in front of me in a whole new light. I tell her about the Love Life on-site testing which will happen the next morning in the mission yard.

"I will do it and I will talk to the others at Mapusha."

I call Regina, Wonder and Susan and ask each to tell others, to tell the women of Tiyiselani. It feels like I am on a surfboard, and the wave is high. After too long watching the ravages of this disease on the community I care about so deeply, it thrills me to see action happening. The slow wheel of change is turning. The women are stepping up to get tested.

I am there first thing in the morning and sure enough, right on time, a white van pulls up. It has no logo and the women who climb out are dressed discreetly in slacks and tan bush shirts. A young man erects two small pup tents in the mission yard. By the time I move into the studio, the guest counselors are already at the table in the corner with the young women. I speak briefly with Regina, but I feel out of place, not part of the ensemble.

Deciding to head out early for Nelspruit I see in my rear view mirror that Gertrude is settled in one small tent with a counselor, and Regina is in the other. A cluster of women is meandering up the path towards the studio and I can't resist beeping my horn and waving, waving as I head down the drive.

I'm curled on the couch with my latest Wilbur Smith novel when Emerencia calls.

"Everyone was tested, Judy, all of the women of Mapusha and all of the Tiyiselani women came as well. And I am negative. You don't know what a stone off my head that is. Always, always I was scared. Scared that the virus had me and my Sampiwe would lose her mama. Now I am happy, I am relaxed and I will guard my negative status with all of me."

"Thank you, Emerencia. Thank you for calling and thank you for being so brave and so honest."

I lie back, enjoying the luxurious sensation of a big win and musing on the nature of change. It happens in its own time and its own way despite my impatience. I don't know if the younger women will share their status with me, but I don't care. They did it, they crossed the river and now it is in their hands.

I can set off for the States high on this success, and relieved that the pressure is off for salaries, as we have gotten the multi-rug order from England. I'm gulping at what awaits me in Portland. Mom's ninety-one-year-old heart is failing and Sal sorely needs some in-house support. Dad, ninety-five, is still sharp as a tack, but his eyes, his ears, his lower back are in bad shape so, as Mom weakens, things are getting more and more difficult at their home.

# Part Four

Stumbling Along

# An Orphan returns

After four weeks in Portland my father died, and then, seven weeks later, came the death of my mother. In the pre-dawn darkness I roll my suitcase out the door of what was their home. I will sorely miss sharing the grieving process with Sally. We will no longer be able to sit on the porch at dusk for the nightly crow fly-over, talking of the past, our parents, the future. Yet, I long to be buffered by the wide skies of Africa, and the co-op needs me back at the rudder.

I travel the ritual thirty-six hours with my earbuds and Leonard Cohen. Last year a friend came and taught the Mapusha women to sing his haunting "Hallelujah." They didn't understand the meaning of most of the words ("He tied her to a kitchen chair?") but they certainly understood the chorus, and sang it with great heart. I hear their voices as I listen to Cohen, feeling my own lonely flavors of "the holy and the broken Hallelujah." The Mapusha women know how to deal with loss and I look forward to being in the studio with them once again.

Riding on the bus from Joburg to Nelspruit, I drink in the vivid purple of the blooming jacaranda trees against the blue of the endless sky. I gorge on the rolling green fields of the highveld with the few big, lonely old trees dotted about. Watching hundreds of small birds rising up out of the fields, I laugh out loud in a way I haven't laughed in a while, the laugh of wonder.

Musing on my passion for this country as the bus rolls along, I have to admit I remain an alien here. As soon as I open my mouth I am identified as an American. Being a woman here and being a woman in Portland are two entirely different experiences. There is nowhere in my whole South African world where I can totally trust, and totally relax as I can with my sister, my brother, Gail and Dahlia.

My parents are gone. It's a lost pillar of support and I shiver at the loneliness that is sure to come in the months ahead. The lop-sided equation is a puzzle to me. It looks from this vantage point as though what goes out and what comes in are skewed. I find such joy in the energy I put out into the world but there seems too little coming into me, personally. Can I equalize things or will the disparity go on and on? Unhappily, I visualize the gap widening.

David greets me at the gas station where the bus parks and hefts my big bags into their latest new car, a pale Mercedes sedan. He is at his most solicitous. He knows the death and grieving process only too well from his time in the States in the '80s. In the kitchen table of my tree house there is a beautiful bouquet of farm-grown birds of paradise on my counter, and fancy little soaps and shampoos and bubble bath bottles surrounding the base of the vase. I hug him, thank him.

I am eager to get up to Rooiboklaagte to see my Mapusha friends and am off the next morning as the sun rises. It is all so familiar driving past White River's tall eucalyptus trees, the wide fields of banana trees on the Hazyview Road. The number of people walking on the sides of the road increases steadily as I approach the township. My attention is pulled gently outwards. My grieving softens its grip in the light of the bright world of skipping school children and one old, old woman walking steadily up the hill with a huge pile of wood on her head. Even if I wanted to stay closeted with my loss it would be impossible. I turn into Acornhoek and drive slowly through the market center, looking from side to side at the people in this, my little corner of Africa. They get into me and, helpless as a flower to the day, I open.

Bumping over the grate and into the mission yard, who do I see sitting on the steps of the studio but little Elena in a red dress with ruffles and bright orange socks. She watches me with round eyes and a solemn mouth. Does she remember me even though I disappeared for four months, a quarter of her life?

"Hello Elena, how are you?"

She smiles and reaches her arms up towards me. I lift her small form and hug her gratefully as we walk through the door of the studio. All of the women stop what they are doing and come over to greet me. Their eyes are filled with warmth and concern as they clasp my hand, and Regina asks that we sit together to honor my parents. There are prayers, and each woman speaks and, of course, they sing and I cry. They are so glad to be with me again, to share grief with their friend.

I tell them that after my father died, my mother decided she wanted to come back to Africa. She wanted to bring my older sister to meet the women of Mapusha. We had plane reservations, I say. And like a Greek chorus, they all shake their heads in amazement.

"But, she was too sick, we had to cancel our tickets." I shake my head. "She did love South Africa and the women of Mapusha".

Anna begins a hymn, and they sing softly with bowed heads. I envision my sisters and my brother as we gathered around my mother's bed, her breath halting and finally stopping altogether. I removed the oxygen mask she so hated from her face. When they came to take her body they took her diamond ring from her finger. I had never seen her without it. I awkwardly touched her naked hand. We all stood as they carried her body from the room.

It is quiet in the big room. Gertrude reaches over and with the edge of her stampi wipes the tears from my cheek. I am the one who needs support right now, and they have the opportunity to comfort me. They have been wanting to sit with me, to share with me the burden of grief. I thank them, bringing my palms together at my heart, yogi style, honoring the light within each. They understand.

Everyone returns to work and I wander around, looking at the goods that are piling up for the international trade show in England in a few months. I will fly to Birmingham in February to assist with sales. Lizbeth and Angy drag out one of the three big rugs they have completed and unfold it for me to view. It is good, a mix of browns, blues and tans, with an African motif of zigzags and diamonds.

I nod my head and tell them, "Good job." I am relieved that this large order has kept them busy while I was gone. They have done well with it in their sturdy, steady, step-by-step way.

At lunchtime I watch the older women lift the prepared balls of white pap from the plastic container to their tin plates and seat themselves on the floor in reaching range of the communal vegetable dishes. Today they eat strips of baked squash, and a container full of the slimy, green morojo, a native plant filled with nutrition, which David has told them is very, very good for them. I notice that now each of the women has a water bottle by her side, another sign that the lessons of David and Neil's workshop live on.

I stop by Wonder as she eats her lunch - a loaf of bread, two bananas and a little plastic container of mango char for flavor. None of the young women ever take time to cook themselves lunch in the morning as their mothers do. I ask how Tiyiselani is doing and how the studio tours are going.

Emerencia has left Mapusha to work in Hoedspruit for another American transplant with a Guggenheim grant. A passel of Americans will be arriving soon and she will be their township contact. It will be good for her, and she is bringing tours to Mapusha now. She was polite enough to tell me that she was leaving, so I don't feel the same betrayal I felt when Syndi and Kamoocho disappeared.

Wonder has stepped up to fill Emerencia's place as tour guide and I am thankful for her sincerity. Syndi was charismatic and Emerencia a talented, feisty firebrand but Wonder has potential for leadership if we can work our way through her shyness barriers.

"Susan doesn't come to the Tiyiselani meetings anymore," she tells me.

I sigh at the fickle attention of her older sister, who spoke with such passion about helping the poorest women of the village and now can't be bothered to go to a meeting.

"And, it is difficult with Emerencia," she adds. "She brings the tourists to the studio but she keeps all the money."

What? Each tourist pays R100 for the tour, the US equivalent of ten dollars. Emerencia keeps that for herself? Mapusha only gets the money from sales?

Wonder nods, she knows as well as I do that it isn't right, but it is difficult for her to speak up. I understand. Yet another confrontation with Emerencia lurks in the near future.

I enjoy my afternoon at the studio, casually sitting with the women, playing peek-a-boo with Elena. It is familiar to stand by Regina's loom and tell her of the memorial service we had for Mom in Philadelphia. She is pleased that my brother and his wife sang a song and enjoys my rendition of "This little light of mine". I tell her I spoke at the service about how much I would miss Mom's bottomless support of me and of the Mapusha cooperative.

Driving back to Blyde at the end of the day, the sun hits the mountains in that special way. I look forward to sitting and talking with Vicki and I am glad to be back in this world. Yet, I recognize the truth that even here in my South African world internally something is altered. The difference is palpable, as though each cell has had to rearrange itself now that the two people who created me are no longer here on earth. It's a dislocation that hovers near deep emptiness.

Several days later, Emerencia walks through the door and I turn to face her in her new faux-leather jacket, sunglasses and fancy shoes. She comes over to greet me, smiling.

"Welcome back Judy. I am so sorry about your parents passing."

We share an awkward hug. Somehow hugs never quite work with the younger women. She moves over to stand by the table where she used to sit with the others. I watch her closely for clues on how to play the confrontation. It is outrageous to me that she gets a salary from her new job, probably topping that of her mother's at the co-op, and still wants to take all the profit from the tour business set up for the benefit of the cooperative. She and Angy are talking now. Angy is a safe place for her to land. I wonder if she will speak to Wonder. She doesn't. This omission tips me over the edge.

I ask her to please come into the storeroom for a moment. She raises her eyebrows at me but obliges, and we move into the little room in the back.

"Yes, Judy?"

Her face is arranged politely, but I can feel the tension in her body. It is much closer to anger than fear.

"I am so happy that the tours are going well. I hear that many people have come to the studio and everyone says you are doing a good job as the tour guide."

She relaxes slightly and smiles. "Yes, my tour business is going very well and it helps Mapusha."

"How do you divide the fees from the tourists?" I ask innocently, not wanting to implicate Wonder, and aware of Regina's difficult position if I go to battle with Emerencia.

"I don't divide the fee. I am the tour guide and the fee is for my services." Her posture hardens and her tone is aggressively defensive.

"But Emerencia, it was Mapusha that set you up in this business, and without the studio you would have no center for your tours. Don't you think the fees belong in part to the co-op?"

We argue and the air gets heated.

"Why are you trying to take my money away, Judy? I need to support my child."

I am stunned at the accusation, incredulous that she has some-how twisted my actions to an assault on her. I grapple to defend myself, claim my love for Sampiwe, her mother and her. I try to explain how hard I work to help Mapusha be sustainable. I can't help reminding her that Mapusha paid her salary for four years, gave her the platform from which to move forward.

She is listening.

"I just want the division of the fees to be fair," I say.

She backs down, and reluctantly agrees to split the fees with Mapusha.

"I know you do love my family, and my child."

The implication is that I don't love her, and at the moment I don't have it in me to try to get her to see how much I care about her as well as Regina, Sampiwe, Kush, and Obry. I thank her for under-standing, for offering to split the fees with the co-op in the future.

She nods her head at me, but I can see the anger still shining in her eyes. I grapple to explain myself, telling her how sad I am that she feels badly treated when I am so proud of her, and want so much for her to succeed. I try to impress her with how much I want Sampiwe to have a good education, and to feel proud of who she is. And, I want Regina and the women of Mapusha to feel secure about their monthly salaries.

"Yes, Judy, I understand and now I must go to see Sampiwe's teacher."

I'm left alone in the little room and distractedly begin ordering the balls of yarn, sorting them more precisely by color, arranging the reds and oranges neatly. Ambrocia comes to the door and asks if I would like a cup of tea. How I appreciate her simple warmth and laughing eyes. She knows I just fought with Emerencia. I go out to talk again with the weavers and enjoy my tea. I know it will take a bit, but I will soon be at peace with the Emerencia confrontation. I have to keep reminding myself how grateful I am for the empowerment she is so ably modeling.

## The Community Beckons

Gail and Stephen have arrived from Oregon for their annual visit, and in my raw state they are the perfect balm. I have lured them to Blyde with lodgings and the promise of community work in Rooiboklaagte. In truth, sometimes I feel like one-hand-clapping in the village, for I have no one with whom to share my challenges. It is so miraculous to me how very little it takes to make such a difference here. It makes me high. This is what I want others to share, the joy of generosity and gratitude patted together into one slobbery, happy ball.

Stephen's an old community type, having built a yurt community in Eugene in pre-Gail days. And Gail and I can enjoy anybody and anything with our well-attuned sensibilities. Our first venture will be to the grade school where Sampiwe is now a student. I have never actually visited Cheue Primary School and this is the perfect moment.

The principal knows of our plan to visit Sampiwe's classroom, but when the three of us enter the school complex it is filled with children in blue uniforms carrying red plastic chairs on their heads as they walk in the direction of a single room. The cement buildings are old, many windows are broken and a glimpse inside an open classroom door shows us that there is nothing on the pitted wall. Somewhat dazed by the sad state of the school, Sampiwe's school, I lead Gail and Stephen towards the door at the end of the building, the school office where the principal resides to alert him of our arrival, as I was strictly advised to do by Emerencia.

The office is the size of a big closet, in Portland terms, with three desks squished into it, each overflowing with papers. Tired old charts hang on the walls, which have big dark splotches where plaster is missing. It is not an inspiring central command post.

We are introduced to the secretary and the assistant principal who says they will be ready for us soon. Back in the courtyard the parade of children continues. The stream is slowing to a trickle and the assistant principal comes to escort us into the room, which has eaten up the children and chairs, and suddenly I understand. It is a full school assembly and we are the entertainment, the star guests.

We are on display in front of the room filled with hundreds of bright-eyed, squirmy, young bodies. Everyone is focused on us. I am paralyzed with the same stage fright I endured during enforced participation in school plays long ago. I'm not an actress, not a performer, and so I do the only thing I can think to say,

"Hello, how are you?"

The response is a thunderous chorus, "I am fine. How are you?"

Every school child knows at least this much English, but now I am stuck. I don't know how to proceed and look desperately at Gail, who is a performer, singer, and musician. She gamely steps forward and starts to teach the children, "Row, row, row your boat." Happily, I follow along and even manage to cover my ears and participate in the round.

The kids are eager and quickly pick up the tune and the words. At the conclusion we clap loudly together, pleased with our song. I ask the children to sing us something of their choice.

They lift the roof with their clear, bright voices in a Tsotho song. We clap and smile, and they clap and smile, and I lock eyes with Sampiwe in the middle of the room. She is the child of my heart, and this school is her school, and it must improv e.

After finally disentangling ourselves from the eager children we walk up the main road, through the village towards the Mapusha studio where our car is parked. Gail and I move back and forth between tears and laughter. It was a joy to make all those kids so happy. Our entertainment seemed so special to these kids which just shows how very little of interest must occur in their school, their lives. We are horrified by the condition of their school and keep remembering the details. One classroom door was missing altogether. There was nothing, absolutely nothing on the dingy walls other than an old blackboard. So many broken, or altogether missing windows signaled the total sense of neglect enveloping this school, where all of the children from Rooiboklaagte begin their education. It is a treat for me to spill and share my feelings with Stephen and Gail. They speak my language, and after this primary school experience they understand why I am so compelled to be here, and so passionate about this small community.

The next day Gail and I teach a cooking class to the Tiyeselani women in Emma the brick maker's, immaculate kitchen. She now wears the widow's black. We have gathered at her house because she is only allowed to visit the home of another widow for the year of her mourning.

We want them to bring garlic into their diet as David and Neil have recommended. We will demonstrate how to use raw garlic in a salad, and how to cook it with spinach.

Susan Mbetsi is there and translates for the women, explaining that a clove of garlic can be very helpful for yeast infections. She makes her point clear by rolling her hips and smiling. language barriers and shyness fall away as we chop and laugh and eat together in the tiny kitchen.

I tell them a church in California is raising money to buy them a fence-making machine. Somehow I can't bear to explain that they will be selling chocolate-covered strawberries at their church on Easter Sunday to raise the money for Tiyiselani. These women couldn't imagine having the money to buy a chocolate covered strawberry. They are wide-eyed at the simple fact that people far away want to help them.

As Susan translates this good news, I watch Emma lower her head, shy in her pleasure, as though no one has ever before given her a gift. She is easily six feet tall and stands as straight and grounded as a tree. She divides our leftovers for her five young children who sit patiently outside in the yard. They are curious about these *mulungas* (whites) in their kitchen. I try to imagine her life here in the village, making bricks to sell, and caring for all her children.

The women have enjoyed their afternoon, and this was a much more manageable experience than the school assembly, but in both cases I am left with the feeling that so much more needs to be done. Too many women have too many children and no way to earn a living.

My day-time world grows bigger and more complex as I increase my efforts in the community, but my trip to the trade show in England makes clear the underside of my reality. Together my aching loneliness, my inadequacies as a marketer and the fact of moving forward into a fifth year of unpaid volunteer work twist about in the wind and are clearly articulated during a truck ride from Birmingham on a cold, rainy night.

## Trade Show in England

It is still dark as I trudge up the snowy street towards the bus station on my way to the trade show. Having spent the whole of yesterday manning Sarah Rose's designated space at the show, I'm dreading another endless day of sitting alone with the rugs, talking mostly with earnest women who are trying to ascertain if these rugs are made under fair labor conditions. I assure them that I get nothing, no money comes my way from the making and sale of these rugs. We pass the fair labor tests with flying colors but it doesn't help sell the rugs.

The little covered bench at the bus stop looks suspiciously empty and there is no one in sight on the streetlamp lit street. It's too cold to wait sitting so I pace back and forth. The new black clogs I bought for the trip are wet and slippery and I am thoroughly miserable walking up and down the block in the dark, waiting for the bus that doesn't come. A hunched form with a dog on a lead is walking in my direction and I move towards him to ask about the bus.

"Oh no, dear! It is Sunday and the buses are quite lean. You would be better off to walk to the train station down the road, take the A train two stops, and then get on the train to the trade center."

Thus begins the first leg of my public transport odyssey. I who famously hate public transportation, know that after my two train rides I will walk through more slush to pick up the shuttle to take me to the G pavilion. Then, once I have arrived in the proper place, I can sit all day and feel people either brush past without a glance or look and leave without a word and then begin the bus, train, and slush walk back to my tiny hotel room.

This is not what I had in mind. There is no glamour in this lonely weekend in a cold, grey England. There is no use trying to sell the too-African looking rugs in one of 27 large pavilions filled with cool, modern, slick or corny English country chintz. Chickens, geese, ducks, lambs and dogs are the motifs of choice here.

The show finally closes, and I spend hours taking everything down and packing it up, and now I am standing next to the big van owned by a friend of Sarah Rose's. The ground is slushy and it is dark as we load the final items in. Joseph tells me I can curl up in back and sleep if I want. It seems preferable to sitting in the front with him. I am in no mood for boring conversation. He likes to talk sports and mechanics.

I try to curl up so that no part of me touches the cold metal of the van. My socks are wet and there is only one dark thought circling in my head, "What are you doing?"

I recall the phone conversation when Sarah Rose broached the idea of my coming to England for the international trade show to represent Mapusha, and my enthusiastic response. I have loved England for as long as I can remember, whether from reading hundreds of English novels or because of an idyllic college summer I spent living in a little bedsitter around the corner from the British Museum. I ate raspberries from the greengrocer each morning, wore wild hats and merrily hitch-hiked alone around the island, but England in February is a different story, and the trade show didn't tickle my design fancy one bit. Shivering, I recall my wander through the Chinese pavilion yesterday. It was filled with endless, cheaper-than-cheap stuff. They sold 'hand woven' rag rugs for one dollar.

The *What am I doing?* mantra runs endlessly, like a Mobius strip. Well, I'm trying to support the weaving cooperative, comes my answer. But as the truck bumps along, I wonder really, why *am* I lying in a cold van on the outskirts of Birmingham England? It is one of those rock-bottom moments. Somehow supporting the women of Mapusha has eclipsed supporting myself and it isn't just a zero sum, this trip is dipping seriously into the negative zone. The bleakness of the situation consumes me.

We sold nothing, or rather Sarah Rose sold nothing and she is now stuck with $5,000 worth of rugs. It was the wrong show for them, but will I ever find the right show? I am much better at getting donations than I am at selling rugs, better as a non-profit fundraiser than a marketer or businesswoman. My inner voice is that cold, hard one, the one that always sounds so sensible. I am a fool to try to be doing this alone, no one in her right mind would do what I do for no pay. I can't afford to be a volunteer any longer.

It has been four years and each month is still a struggle. The voice goes on and on. It seems to speak in perfect sync with the bumps and rumbles of the old van as we speed through the dark night.

## The Good, the Bad and the Many Questions

Soon after my black moment in the Birmingham van comes more than enough help on the community front to keep me hopping. It is as though a pipeline opens and support flows into Rooiboklaagte. I enlarge my sphere and begin work on the creche and the grade school, continue with the women of Mapusha and the women of Tiyiselani. I pull in Jean, a wonderful new friend from my yoga classes in White River, and she in turn pulls in a slew of super-efficient mothers from the private school that her sons attend. The web of support for the projects continues to expand. Yet, more support means many new jobs for me. I am at over-full capacity writing emails and thank-you notes, ordering wool, considering construction at the grade school, teaching weekly art classes to teams of Cheue kids in the mission yard, fundraising and generally making things happen.

We are still unable to find a local market for Mapusha's weavings and have again turned to the States for sales and support. Too often it is the donations that get Mapusha through the year. Steady monthly salaries are so important to the women and their 65 dependents. It is 2008, my sixth year in Africa. Elena grows, Sampiwe morphs into an adolescent and Anna Mduli has her power back. Gertrude and Regina remain my stalwart duo as we pilot our way through the various terrains. Emerencia continues to become more and more empowered, and continues to spar with me.

I ache with a hunger for home when I miss the election of Barack Obama. While he is being elected I am sitting on the deck of Vicki's lodge with a baboon troop in the nearby trees and impala grazing on the lawn. Miraculously, the Internet is functioning and I listen as Pennsylvania, my home state, is called for Obama. This man I so admire and trust is our new president, and I am sitting far away with only baboons and impalas for companions.

I went to the studio that Election Day bringing celebratory cinnamon buns and the women cheered when I walked through the door. As I made my rounds of the room distributing the goodies, each woman raised her fist in a power salute and said, "Obama!". They seemed to understand my support of this man and, as Regina said, "You must feel proud today as I did the day Nelson Mandela was elected."

It is to the Mapusha studio I go to be quiet and to be nourished by their steady, stable presence and the whir of the spinning wheel. Sitting by Regina's loom one day I watch the colors flow and mingle with each other in her current tapestry. I can lose myself in her abstract color weavings. She is attuned to subtle beauties and deep truths. I remember watching her watch the bush world going slowly dark as we drove out of Kruger Park last year. It was a special outing for the cooperative. Funds were collected when I told a living room full of Portland Quakers that these women had never been to Kruger Park, though it was on the doorstep of their homes, 30 kilometers down the road. The funds were raised for everything from transport to picnic food --kilos of chicken and wurst to braai (grill) for lunch.

That day we met at the studio early in the morning. Everyone was dressed to the hilt. Wonder wore a shiny black gown. Each woman had her particular brand of special shoes and special hats for our day in the park. Perhaps they enjoyed the food even more than the animals we saw. And we saw many -- dazzles of zebra in an open field with their wildebeest friends, herds of gentle impala and a single smiling hyena sauntering down the side of the road.

After lunch we all climbed into an open vehicle provided by the park, complete with a Tsotho-speaking guide. I watched the women watch this bush, their natural world, as we drove slowly along. A lilac-breasted roller perched on a tree branch, and spider webs decorated the tall grasses with their glistening fiber creations.

Regina's face stays with me. Regina taking in the greens of the trees and the grasses through which we moved reminded me of someone returning home after a long absence. The beauty she was seeing all around her was somehow what she had always known. It was the world she had imagined within herself. Now it was reflected in the bushveld of the park, and she kept quietly nodding as if saying, "it is right, it is as it should be."

After that day her weavings become even more subtle and complex color blendings. They seemed to hold a sense of the South African world in its most harmonious splendor. Angy, admiring Regina's style, becomes a weaver who specializes in abstract color musings, too.

If Regina and Angy are the artists, Lindy and Lizbeth are the designers of all things Mapusha. Lindy was the oldest of 13 children and Lizbeth was nearly the youngest. Lindy has been weaving for 42 years and Lizbeth since 2003, but they both are talented and my goal with them is to somehow provide them with the materials and the freedom to grow.

Quiet Lindy is a master of design. She always draws her own templates and carefully chooses the colors, dyes them if need be. It is inevitably a surprise to me what comes forth. Sometimes it is fanciful flowers with floating impalas and zebras, and sometimes it is a wonderful abstract geometric composition. The younger women once told me she could make any dress in their fancy dress magazines and I believe it. She sews school uniforms at night and is always impeccably turned out. I have never given her a single piece of advice after the time I returned from a trip to the States and saw what she had created in my absence. The first tapestry she ever wove of her own design was of the mountains of the Drakensburg with the Blyde River curving through the base of the canyon. It has been a joy to watch her truly spread her wings as a weaver. Her tapestries have gotten increasingly sophisticated, fanciful with the freedom to do as she will. She is a silent master, and I dream of her having a one-woman show somewhere, somehow.

Lizbeth, too, is a natural designer and, in the best of all possible worlds, she would go to school and hob-nob with other designers, but she has a child and a household of siblings with children.   She works in geometrics and colors and creates things that delight me, and surprise me, whether a tapestry or a small woven bag with a big felt button. She always adds a sparkle of fun as well as beauty to her pieces, she has a younger, more contemporary eye than the others. I buy her Lowveld Living design magazines and she pours over them.

Mapusha will be having a show at a museum in Tillamook, Oregon next year featuring tapestries and rugs, mobiles and photos of the women and their world. The studio is a petri dish of self-expression. Self-expression is empowerment, and empowerment of these women is what I have wished for them from the day I met them. I turn back to admire the way Regina has brought a deep blue into the woven flow of greens.

## Cheue Primary gets a Facelift

It seems, here in my African world of community development as though all things good unfold in due time. I bring my attention to something, call its name and activity magically begins to happen. This is the way it is with Cheue.

The night after our *Row, Row, Row Your Boat* experience I sent pictures of the school to my sister, Sally. She teaches in an elementary school on the outskirts of Portland, and when others in her staffroom see the pictures they immediately decide to do a penny-drive for Cheue. Overnight it is organized and each class is tasked with raising money. Various schemes emerge. One teacher says he will shave his head if his students can raise $100.

On my next visit home I am the special guest at a whole school assembly where two young girls hand me a check for $3,000. The teacher shaves his head. I try to convey to these American children what their gift will mean to the children in Africa. I try to tell them about the broken windows that will be fixed, the walls that will be painted and the blackboards that will be installed. I tell them the children will be proud of their school. I thank them.

After the penny-drive success in Portland, I am back at the Mapusha studio, working with Wonder to spiff up the storeroom on a Saturday before the co-op returns from their Christmas break. Stephen and Gail have returned to the States, and the project of painting the storeroom has risen to the top of my long to-do list. We have hopes of getting more tourists to come to the co-op to meet the women of Mapusha and see their wares. Since we have no local market this is the only way to stop relying on sales in America. When Wonder's phone rings I give it little thought until she hangs up and tells me Emerencia's top lodge is sending some tourists to Mapusha. Tourists, now? And Emerencia cannot come to greet them. We will greet them. There is nothing for them to see other than me in my ragged shorts and an old shirt with holes, significantly worse than my usual wear, which is none too great either. The storeroom is pulled apart and the weavers are all at home planting their corn. I look with alarm at Wonder who is trying to remember the name they said, the name of the guest.

"Elton John," she recalls.

Elton John is coming? What? This puts me in full panic mode. Wonder shrugs. They are leaving the lodge now and will be here in half an hour. I scramble around trying to make the studio look presentable, draping the empty looms with some of the weavings piled on the floor. I call Regina and Gertrude and beg them to come up.

The white van pulls in the driveway and immediately various well-dressed folks pile out. Regina, Gertrude, Anna Mbetsi and Anna Mduli have all made it there in time and are wearing bright kerchiefs and Shangaan shawls. They take the hands of their visitors and greet them gracefully. It seems Elton John himself has not come, but this group is his New Year's party group, his close friends from London and New York. They enter the torn-apart studio and laugh with me as I explain it is planting time for the women, that we are painting, and on and on. Regina asks if they would like to see the church and we go in and kneel together on the simple wooden benches as Gertrude says a prayer.

As the bus prepares to return to 5-star luxury I stand in the mission yard talking with a blonde woman who seems deeply touched by her experience with the women. Her husband makes jewelry for Elton John and she is a designer. She simply asks what is needed and I say, boldly, a borehole at Cheue to provide water for the children to drink and the women to make a big garden. She immediately, simply states she will do it and she does. Returning to the lodge, over drinks she asks all of her group to donate for the borehole at Cheue. We have the money within a month, and I find myself now managing a borehole project.

The final grand topping on this project comes when my increasingly good friend Jean decides she will come to Cheue over a weekend with her friends and all their children. This will be her son Matt's project, and it spurs a flurry of activity at Cheue. All 12 of them (3 mothers, 9 children) come down for a weekend and together we decorate the outside walls of Cheue with colorful handprints. The White River children begin painting the hands of the excited Cheue students but soon it is a total mélange, and the result is a wondrous mesh of small hands in many colors dancing across the entrance walls to the schoolyard.

Cheue has a facelift and everyone is pleased.

It is no different with our little nursery school, the Katlego creche. A fiery and competent new volunteer is running the school and it is thriving. There are donations from many. Now the classroom has glass windows and security doors, a raft of small brightly-colored plastic chairs and tables. This is where I bring all visitors, for the eagerness and laughter of the 30 children under five never fails to delight. It is a pleasure for me to watch the children sing for the visitors, or vice versa. They play ball, do art projects with the children.

Dieter is a recently retired man, originally from Germany. He tells me he doesn't know how to play with the children, doesn't know how to help. Then he has an idea. He has me drive him to the building supply store and he buys wood that is cut into block-size rectangles. He takes these blocks to the creche and sits on the outside step, methodically sanding each block. The children surround him, and watch him carefully. They have never seen blocks before. They want to help him, and he lets the bravest young boy put his hand on his own as he sands the wood.

Finally, he is done and carries the dozens of smoothed blocks inside. The children don't know what to do with them. One child hits another on the head with a block and I gasp. But slowly, slowly they learn. The blocks over time become even smoother from the children's hands as they create walls, houses and walkways.

Another family brings art supplies for the pre-schoolers. Francesca, 15 years old and often filled with all of the self-centered angst of teenagedom, becomes a genuinely generous being when she works with the kids. Standing at the side of the plastic table, I watch as she helps a small girl put a particularly stubborn bead on a plastic string. Her face looks so smooth and lovely, without any crinkles of dissatisfaction.

My joy these days is my time in Rooibok with the creche children, my art class of Cheue children and, of course, the women of Mapusha. Tension is arising in my relationships with both David and Leslie and though Vicki remains my steadfast buddy she is newly involved with a young crowd of dancing, barhopping friends. It isn't my scene and holds little interest for me. When I am not at the studio or involved in some Rooibok project, I am usually reading a book on whatever bed I inhabit for the night, either in Vicki's spare room at the Blyde lodge or at the farm.

## Art Class

I am always happy to see the uniformed grade school kids trooping up the path into the mission yard for my weekly, after-school art class. Wonder assists me with the 40 or so children as we paint and draw and make homemade play dough.

On nice days we take our supplies outside, but on rainy days an empty room at the bottom of the mission yard serves as our base.

The kids sit on the floor, entranced by their projects with crayons, paints and whatever I might find or dream up for them. I teach in my loose, do-as-you-will way and blog each week about my art class experiences.

One art class day it is raining hard, which could possibly keep everyone home. But, at the specified time the children charge into our empty room with enthusiasm. Twenty children between the ages of six and ten are taking off their coats and backpacks to sit unencumbered on the floor. Unfortunately, Wonder is down with the flu so it is just me with my English, the children with their Tsonga, and ten packets of brightly colored tissue paper.

One by one I open the packets. Suspense builds in the classroom. I can feel the longing of the children for something new. I lift my arm high in the air and walk slowly, slowly round the room. Finally I let a bright filmy sheet drift from my hand. The whole room watches the purple paper float towards the floor. Their eyes widen with this very unteacherlike action, but they quickly catch the mysterious mood and begin to reach for the sheets with wide smiles.

I show them how to rip them up to create a pile of tissue pieces. I show them the little glue containers, and mime gluing their tissue pieces to their own piece of construction paper. Make a picture, I say over and over, trying to imprint the English words on them. I know in my bones that to create something helps them to believe in themselves. Each week it is an exercise in empowerment through the right-brain, which is so alive in these bright youngsters.

Soon that special, wonderful silence of children absorbed in their creations fills the room. This is what I plan, prepare and aim to create. It is the delicious, short space within each class when the children loose themselves in a world of color and the play of creating something.

Elena is the youngest in the class. Though just three and a half years old, she understands. Sampiwe sits helpfully by her side, tearing the red and yellow tissue into little pieces. Elena carefully, with the fingers of her grandmother Lindy, begins to glue each bit down onto her bright red paper.

One shy young girl is making flowers with her tissue pieces, flowers such as grow neither in her yard nor in the village. I reflect on how little color touches their world between the treeless roads and raked yards, the roaming goats, the lack of water. I bend to tell her "beautiful, beautiful" and clap my hands in praise.

At the end of the class I walk the whole gang up to Mapusha, and the women surround them, praising their work. The children duck their heads, hiding their shy, happy pride, then run out of the studio on their way home, holding tight to their art work.

I say good-bye to each of the women and head back to Nelspruit. This is my weekly rhythm now. I drive up at dawn on Mondays to the studio and spend Monday and Tuesday nights with Vicki at her lodge in the canyon, and then drive back to my tree house at the farm in Nelspruit for the long weekend to dye wool, do accounts, and write emails and blogs and Mapusha newsletters.

The two-hour drive is a time for the simple cheer of John Prine or the primal ache of Lucinda Williams on my iPod. Or I play with plans, visions, daydreams, and duties in my head. The Birmingham-born inner voice of cold reason and caution regarding my choices never completely disappears. It natters and nags. I shoo it away but can never quite banish it with the necessary authority. This alter ego of my courageous *Jump!* persona usually takes a backseat to my enthusiasm about all that is in motion at the Mapusha studio, the Katlego Creche and the Cheyu primary school. But it hovers nearby, always.

On the farm I have had my first real out-and-out fight with David. We sat, we yelled, and in the end we agreed to disagree. But, what I learned is what I feared. We don't follow the same rulebook. I bank on being as honestly vulnerable as possible to get me through any kind of conflict or misunderstanding with my friends. David has a different idea. He attacks to cleanse himself of unwanted stress. Anyone receiving one of his cleansing diatribes is to deal with it as he does, and move on from it as he does. If I have a problem it is my problem. Vulnerability is not part of his equation. He expresses, he lets go, he forgives. But honest vulnerability, no.

Sometimes I take his words, eat them and burn with the shame of them. Sometimes I ignore them, act as if they aren't worthy of my attention, and sometimes I fight back. I'm glad I can fight back and hold my own, but I wish I didn't have to. The dream of a family of choice at the farm is becoming seriously tarnished.

I pull into the garage to see my cat, Mia, sliding along the porch wall, welcoming me home. I smell the blooming jasmine and am glad to be back on the hill with the rustling Nebalm trees and my beloved pet.

## Heartening

Increasingly, I delegate authority to Wonder, entrusting more and more tasks and duties to her. She is building her own home and running a subsidiary business under the Mapusha roof, assisted by an artist from Hoedspruit. She is growing her own voice and enjoys leading the tourist tours of the studio, the creche, and the village. She works well with both the older and the younger women at the studio. Though never a weaver herself, she now sits at the studio with Ambrocia, making the bright mobiles popular with our visitors. And she is the acknowledged chairwoman of Tiyiselani.

One cool day I stand in Emma's empty garage watching Wonder lead the others in assembling the new fence-making machine. It has finally arrived from Swaziland after innumerable emails, phone calls and glitches. Rolls of wire are stacked to one side. This wire should be transformed first to fencing and then to cash for the women of Tiyiselani in the days and weeks to come.

Wonder is the leader, and she does it well in this prickly woman's world with its many underground rules. I am just the cheerleader today; bringing cookies and watching them work together with the metal circles and rods.

The fence-making machine works. The women take turns circling the handle of the roller and, magically, entwined wire is created. Their triumph is palpable. It seems as though the final piece is in place. I imagine these women beginning to earn a salary, order the wire, keep the books, and create a successful business. I put an imaginary check by the Tiyiselani project.

Emma is carefully oiling various joints when Wonder comes over to tell me about the school meeting she attended as the Tiyiselani representative the day before. The principal wanted to control the money donated to Cheue from America and Wonder stood up and said, "No. Tiyiselani will be the mother of the money."

I'm impressed. As she walks back to smooth some dispute over the proper way to adjoin this piece with the other, the image of her when she first came to the studio flashes before me. She had two girls and no husband. She had been selling small snacks to the school children from the side of the road before she became an apprentice at Mapusha. Her shyness was painful, but she persisted, and here she is today.

I consider another of the apprentices, Emerencia, who now works in the administration at Cheue and is busy championing the poorest of the poor children. Angy and Lizbeth are the weavers and they are good. Mapusha is now selling their work to tourists and maybe this is the angle we have always needed into the local market, a way to sell to the non-locals.

I stroll past Cheue with its new gate and thriving garden. The painted handprints on the walls of the school are beginning to fade, but they are happy hands. Small boys on the side of the road wave and call out my name. They are Cheue students these days, but I knew them when they were toddlers at the creche. My heart is full as I consider how well my adopted village is doing.

## On Top of the Canyon

Snaking around the smooth curves of the steep road towards the top of the Blyde River Canyon, I exhale long and slowly to help me feel into the wide breadth of these green covered hills. They roll out before me against the sky. I tingle with an aching love for this land, and yet I feel I'm being pushed out. I'm still smarting from the latest hard knock from David, hurting from my break with Leslie, and genuinely discouraged about my inability to support myself in this world. I'm hoping this high vantage point will offer at least a glimpse of new perspective.

When perched on a lichen-covered boulder at the very edge, I soften my eyes to the river curling through the base of the canyon below and let my mind float. The 'river of joy' ripples through my lonely self and I am back at the farm, having a conversation with David about a house sitter for Mia while I return to the States for Christmas. He told me about his dear friend who would stay with my Mia cat, but only if he could use my car, and only if I paid half the utilities. It is a skewed deal and I know it. David's friend is getting a free ride in exchange for feeding my cat, but David is pleased.

I felt a sinking sensation when I heard the terms of his arrangement. I was the loser and with this small action what I had been suspecting seemed confirmed. I was being quietly pushed out of the tight inner-circle status at the farm. I still had dinner with the boys, but we watched the news instead of talking and I was back in my tree house with Mia by 6 pm. Now, their big wooden front door is often closed, David's temper is shorter, and Neil's abstracted air more complete. If I were a bigger person I probably wouldn't bother to take it personally or I might wonder what I was doing differently, but in this case, in my semi-starved state, it hurts. Leopard Tree Retreat will never be the cozy commune of high-minded activists and artists that I had once imagined. Communal living isn't a good fit with these two. They don't want a third, a fourth or any other wheel at their show. They are complete, two is perfect, thank-you. I understand this, but I have a raft of tender bruised pockets at my core.

With Leslie, too, there is bruising, loss and disappointment. The image I see is the thin cord of trust between us finally snapping. The details of the conflict melt away, and the raw sense of being truly separated from her remains. I understand why she doesn't trust me, for I do hide thoughts and feelings from her as she suspects. But, whether I hide things because I don't want to hurt her or because I don't want to be hurt by her is still an open question and maybe that is the good news, an actual sign of new life. It isn't a given this time with either of these people, to each of whom I gave authority status in years past, that I'm the wrongdoer. I am bruised but not broken, sad but not shamed. I wasn't silent in the confrontational moments and did not swallow the criticisms whole. Is it enough?

The wind whips my hair back and I am reminded of how my scalp hurt when my hair first fell out. It ached with the vulnerability of exposure. Dahlia took me to a creek bed on a summer's day and put damp moss on my head to soothe the hurt to my pride and to my head. This was just days after the bald mirror moment when I saw myself as a shamed and powerless woman. I arrived here in the lowveld eight years ago with that image foremost in my mind, but it has faded, and now comes the memory of my bald head and the soothing moss.

Here, I have no Dahlia to cover me with moss, but I'm no longer caught in the sinkhole of helplessness as I was then. Nor am I shrinking from the world. I feel closer on the scale of things to one of those bald Buddhist nuns whose wrinkled faces always seem to smile with the warm acceptance of what is. I'm not exactly smiling but I'm not cowering in my own vulnerability.

Tiring of my rock perch, I stand to take in my grand view of the bushveld, the rivers, and the sculptures of ancient rocks. I'll have to find inspiration alone to tackle the problems in my world now. I must find a well of possibility within rather than looking outside for help. David and Leslie were beacons for me around and through the cancer dance. Their bright vision was here, in this land, amidst these people, when I needed it most. They helped me to jump but they are no longer my beacons. I feel a big gulp of loss in the very center of my being.

In a Kundalini move I shake my hands and imagine the old energies of looking outside myself for truth flying out through my fingertips, floating down on the winds of the canyon. I close my eyes and imagine a world without the big people, the ones I run to when there is a snake in my house, the ones who will have the answers when I don't. Following the path around the edge of the cliff I try to doff the mantle of aloneness and let myself join into this top of the world spot but my mind spins on, circling and wondering about the gifts and the pitfalls of my fluid nature. I have learned much from being close to Leslie and to David.

There is always the issue of my longing for a nest. Mom and Dad are gone, another vanished safety nook. The sun goes behind a cloud. Just me. There are no whispers of wisdom from the kachina of the canyon, but maybe that is just as it should be.

Gradually, reluctantly, my dial moves towards retreat, return to the comforts of Portland and be a grown up, make a living. David and Neil reclaim my house at the farm four years ahead of the terms of our original agreement — a 10-year lease in exchange for the money I put into the renovations. I have no choice. Either I pay the monthly utility fees or I let my tree-house go. I pack up my books and my chotskies. I ship several boxes of my favorite things back to Portland. Vicki's son retrieves the Pygmy bed that has been my alter, the lamp made of veld wood with the wild shade of coarse burlap, my beloved carved leopard. Vicki will keep them for me, hold a space for me here, take charge of my car, and closet a bag of my favorite battered bush clothing.

I give away clothes, art supplies, and kitchen utensils. Trips to Goodwill are unnecessary in this reality where so many need so much. I can fill a cardboard box with almost anything and it will be emptied and appreciated within hours.

An educational elder hostel group from Portland comes to the co-op in the last month of my time in Rooibok and together we have one of those magical times. We visit the creche and the friendly three and four-year-olds capture their hearts with their songs, their smiles. The women of Mapusha greet these elders with open arms and their own songs. One woman has brought head scarves in very American calico prints for each of the women. Many pictures are taken. Returning to their lodging, they decide to join forces and attempt to help the cooperative, to try to make a difference. They envision a marketing brochure, a new website. I hold onto this with a tight grip, hoping beyond hope that this lifeline will help the women when I leave. I envision working for Mapusha despite being in

Portland, helping to create a wonderful website, using Skype to call Wonder and check on wool orders. Maybe I'll write my story, and maybe that will help the women somehow. It scalds my throat to think of leaving but leaving I am.

## Last Day at the Co-op?

Emma is the first to arrive at our party. It is my final day at the co-op and I've invited the women of Tiyiselani to join us for tea and cookies. I shake hands with Emma and express how happy I am to see her wearing colors again, the official mourning for her husband complete. As she takes a seat on the bench I remember all the different scenes of which she has been a part —— helping to assemble the new fence-making machine in Lena's garage, working with Stephen to place new window panes in the kindergarten at Cheue, hostessing our cooking class where Gail and I taught them the wonders of garlic. Others arrive and the cookies are carefully divided into small piles, one pile for each of the attendees.

Wonder is my translator. I explain that I must return to America for the rest of the year. I lift my hand and rub my thumb against my fingers and they understand that I need money and so, of course, I must return to America where they know money is easy.

"I ask you women to continue our work with the garden at Cheue, the creche, the neediest in your community. You will have to do my work as well. I will be far away but I will always be thinking of you, hoping that you are well and Rooiboklaagte is getting stronger and stronger as a community."

There is silence but they seem to understand.

Regina thanks me for my help and then asks that we pray together and thank God for his help to the community and the cooperatives.

So, for one last time I sit with eyes leaking tears as I listen to the prayers of the women, the Tsonga sounds so faith-imbued. I am soothed, almost cradled by the sound of the words, as I near one of those goodbyes that are always so difficult for me. They sing together and then stand and begin the *'Thank you'* song with which we have always ended every tour to the studio. As they sing, they circle the room and each woman shakes the hands of the visitors, only this time the visitor is me.

I shake their hands, one by one. The warmth, the love in the eyes of one after the other has me in full meltdown, which makes them smile. They know me. They will miss me coming in the door of the studio with new ideas and surprises for them.

I talk to Wonder about the art class and the fence-making endeavor that she will have to run in my absence. Slowly over time it is Wonder who has become my right hand woman. I am proud of how she has grown and developed from a woman too shy to lift her eyes to one who can speak her mind in public with power when she so chooses. She is building her own house now and I promise to save her some kitchen utensils from my home.

All of the women stand on the steps waving good-bye to me. Elena runs out for a final 'farewell sweetie' from my hand through the open car window. I toot and wave and cry and hope they will be all right in my absence. Then I have to laugh at myself. If there is one thing these women know to do it is to keep on keeping on despite losses, despite obstacles, despite no money.

I drive through Acornhoek, past the market and the blaring music and the wily goats, wondering how will I get myself back here.

# Part Five

RESOLUTION

# WORKSHOP LEAVINGS

R ain drizzles in the near dark of dusk as Gail and I pack our cars with the detritus of our workshop, stuffing the bags and bundles, yoga mats and pillows into the back. We huddle together beneath an umbrella before she heads off for dinner with Stephen and I head back to feed the cats at my new Portland home.

I can only shrug, and she agrees with a nod. We tried to teach and inspire the ten participants with our thoughts and exercises. It was okay, Gail tries to tell me, but I feel flat, and I shouldn't feel flat after a day of teaching. Teaching should be uplifting and inspiring. The core of my teaching has always been about faith, courage, confidence. The task is to inspire the participants. But maybe it isn't possible to inspire others when I'm not inspired myself. Saying the words, teaching the concepts isn't the point, really. Is it?

Gail and I agree to talk in the morning, hoping for a fresh perspective on the day's work. I drive home with the windshield wipers toiling to keep the window clear and with an undeniable sense of the thick, flat stratus cloud just above my head.

The house is cold and the cat's hungry, but finally I am free to curl myself in a blanket on the couch and consider things properly.

First on the list is to curse the day when Joe talked me into renting his house while he moved down to Guatemala to live with his twenty-four year old girlfriend.

I spent hours, days, weeks, cleaning and clearing to convert his cluttered man-cave into a home into which I could welcome clients and friends. I enjoyed my 2nd-hand store search for the sweetly embroidered lace curtains in the dining room windows, the heavy orange silk ones in the living room closing out the din of 82nd Ave. But now that is done and here I sit on the couch with one skittish cat and another who likes to gorge and then vomit on the rugs.

I don't really mind the neighborhood. I buy sugar-sprinkled pastries at the Mexican grocery around the corner, get the oil changed by the Russian mechanics across the street, and walk to the Ma and Pa store down the block where the Asian man takes my money, but seems to speak no English. He only nods as I come and as I go. A police siren speeds by and Shadow, Joe's feral find, spooks and runs for her window exit into the dark, wet, people-free safety of the night. This just isn't working. I have my own home, the cats, the car, clients, and my tried-and-true Sunday yoga class but it all feels off, off target, off center, off.

It's not just that I desperately miss Mapusha and the feel of my South African world. I do. I try to assuage that by working harder on their new website, or calling Wonder more often on Skype, or planning a visit in late November. No, the bigger problem is that I can't help feeling as though my work there isn't complete. If there were a trailer across the bottom of my brain screen, it would say, "Mission incomplete." It might add, "Judy wimped out".

Ichero jumps up and plops his large scab-scarred body by my side. I scratch behind his ears gently as I consider the fact that, somehow, I let my little fears and niggling doubts run the show. I know that nothing can really sing when fear is at the helm. I betrayed the bottom line basis of all I teach - trust yourself, take a leap, lead with your heart. How could I have let the whispers of fear fill my head, the tyranny of the practical pull me back to get safe, get secure? I extricate myself from the blanket and the cat to head for bed, glad that I'm now clear on what is and isn't happening and why, though I'm still utterly unclear about what to do.

## The Call

A few weeks later as I'm driving to the local Whole Foods store on a rainy autumn day, day-dreaming with delight about my departure from this too-grey world in a couple of weeks, the familiar T-Mobile ring tone sounds and, reaching with one hand, I retrieve the cell from the bottom of my purse as I pull to the side of the pretty tree-lined street.

"Becky?" I am surprised and suddenly nervous to hear the voice of my good friend who lives at Blyde as CEO of Seeds of Light. She is my main conduit of news from the Rooiboklaagte community and we send emails back and forth and chat on Skype but a call to my cell signifies something different.

She cuts straight to the chase, "I have two pieces of bad news for you, Judy."

Bad news from Africa is more likely to be deadly serious than bad news from Portland. She relates that Wonder is very sick, in the hospital, and the doctor says it is 50/50 she will make it. My mind races as she continues to tell me the details of the doctor's visit. How could it be? Is it AIDS? But she was tested, and I never heard of any men in her life. Oh no, not Wonder, please, please not Wonder.

"They have her on a drip and on antibiotics. We are all praying and I'll keep you informed."

I tell her to give my love to Gertrude, Wonder, everyone in the family and we discuss what we can do to help before I dare ask about the second piece of bad news.

It seems the new Father at the mission has told the Mapusha women they must pay R800 ($80.00) a month rent and that they will be evicted from the building in 2014.

"What?"

Everything goes into slow motion as I try to digest this information. First Wonder and now the Mission Father is threatening Mapusha. It feels like everything is tumbling down over there, and the helplessness of sitting in this car thousands of miles away makes me sick to my stomach. Who is this guy? This new Father must not understand the thirty-six year bond between the mission and the cooperative. He doesn't yet see that the women have been the stewards of the church for years and years. It has always been a give-and-take and the women are proud of their deep connection to this church. It is the church they attend daily and have since they were schoolgirls. It is what has gotten them through the hard times.

Becky explains that he is from Mexico, and I groan inwardly remembering the male and females roles in the land where I traveled so often with Joe.

I ask Becky if she thinks they can stand up to him. She is doubtful and suggests that Nick, her assistant, go to talk to him, man-to-man.

My eyes roll at the clash of the African male-dominated culture with the Mexican male-dominated culture with the Roman Catholic male-dominated culture. She promises to keep me informed but I am inwardly swirling as I drive on to the store. I am mentally composing an email to the new Father. It must be a case of misunderstanding.

And Wonder, oh Wonder, please don't leave. My mind goes back to her sister Peddy's death. I don't think I can handle watching Gertrude lose a third daughter and the thought of Caleb losing another mother makes me shiver.

I do what I can do stateside and chafe to get over there. I write an impassioned letter to the priest whose name I still do not know and send it to Becky. She is more professional and politic than I, and I want her to make sure my tone is not too strident. I couldn't bear it if my actions made things worse for the women, but I felt I had to try to explain. He must know how close to the edge the co-op is financially and he must understand how many thousands of dollars of donations for Mapusha have gone into making the building what it is today -- the new roof, the secure store room, the new bathroom. I professed the hope that we could work this through in a way that worked for everyone.

That is all true but my deepest pain is for the women, who, I now know feel, as I feared they would, very sad about their current relationship with the mission. I spoke with Regina on Skype and I could just see her shaking her head in helplessness as she talked to me. When the Father received my email he stormed over to the studio and stood yelling at her since I was unavailable. Seems I didn't honor his position enough. I pale to think of the scene, just what I didn't want to happen. I assured her I would be there in two weeks and fume at this priest who does understand the situation and doesn't seem to care.

I write emails and ask the 'Friends of Mapusha' network we have built over the years for support. I don't go as wild as I could for I still have hope that once I can talk to this man face-to-face there will be a way to work it through. Or, I can take Regina and Gertrude on a pilgrimage to the White River office of the Bishop and appeal to him. We could find the original Fathers who started the cooperative and have them testify that the building was built by and for the poor women of the community. I could write articles about the Catholic church mistreating the poor rural women of a village in South Africa or rally the forces of the White River community with all their power and pull. I am full of ideas and beyond eager to get over there.

Soon Wonder is out of the hospital, but Becky reports she is very thin. I wouldn't recognize her she says ominously. I look forward to bringing my cheerleading energies to the cause, and to doing everything I can to help her heal. The hospital has lost the test results so this is task number one, find out her HIV status. Oh, the relief of knowing I will soon be there to fight for the women and to encourage them to fight for themselves.

## Back to Slay the Tyrant

When I walk into the studio the women greet me with great warmth but I can feel the weight of their problems with the mission. It reminds me of the way my head feels when I wake in Portland and the low-pressure system seems to block my connection to the sky. Regina's eyes look confused and heavy with sadness. She shows me the copy of what the Father had her sign in his office one day after a three-hour conversation. I shake my head, this just isn't right.

He gave her two options. Mapusha must pay R800 a month, or R1,000 a month, and Mapusha is evicted in 2014 or 2015. She shrugs with the memory and I feel myself retract in sympathy with her position. How can she fight the head priest?

Wonder has come for the first time in three weeks, and I hug her and congratulate her on her recovery. She is quietly sitting at the table sewing with Ambrocia. I know she is using all the energy available to her just to be here, no energy for chit-chat and extraneous gestures. It almost looks to me as though her head is too heavy for her thin neck but she is here working, and that is proof to me that she is going to fight. I sit next to her and ask quietly if she has gotten tested.

She shakes her head no, but raises her eyes to face me and says, "I will. Not yet but I will." But we need to know, you know we need to know, and I nod my head towards Anna Mduli as a model for the wonder of the anti-retroviral drugs. Wonder nods, she knows but still, I'm troubled by her passivity.

On my third visit to the studio I know instantly something is up. Regina stands from her loom to come towards me.

"The new Father came this morning and wants to see you."

Gertrude and all three Anna are watching me closely and, though I instantly tense upon hearing that my meeting with my nemesis is at hand, I tell them stolidly, "Okay, I'll go talk to him."

I head into the storeroom where Nick is on the computer, trying to get the records straight for Mapusha. He is the new Seeds of Light volunteer, hired by the co-op with funds from a Paul Newman grant to help with accounting. He is his usual utterly calm, focused, unflappable self and I wish that I could somehow manifest his personality for this interview.

Becky suggested I take him, being male, with me to speak with the Father but I am embarrassed to be so lacking in courage. Only a real chicken would ask him to come along. I stand for a minute as he works, and try to compose myself. I don't want to lose it with this Father. I don't want to scream at him. That is what makes me tense, the fear of letting my anger loose on him and somehow making things worse for the women. I guess it's better than fearing the paralysis of shame but it still rests on fear.

I walk through the gate of the electric fence that separates the mission house from the mission yard and knock with feigned confidence on the hollow, wooden door. A big African Father in a grey cossack answers the knock, hears my request, and goes to tell the Father he has a visitor. Father Felipe appears, slightly rumpled. He was probably napping. Short, as I had guessed. His hair is coiffed, and I look down into his dark eyes, as I suspected I would. They are hard, not much light and not much give. He asks that I return in ten minutes to meet him in his office.

I walk back towards the coop, stopping to examine the big orange flowers of the flame tree that have fallen like dotted taffeta over the lawn. He didn't seem like a formidable foe, but the feel of my nerves takes me back to grade school when my stern fifth grade teacher called me in for a private interview. I walked down the long cement corridor of the school towards that meeting taking tiny baby steps, going as deliberately as I could go. When I arrived she berated me in stinging words about my being a leader, but leading in the wrong direction.

The anticipation of meeting this Father has a similar scent. I feel as though I'm awaiting judgement, criticism, condemnation but I don't get it. How could he be in a position to judge me? It seems so obvious to me that his desire to evict the women of Mapusha from the studio after thirty-six years is the action that merits condemnation, doesn't it? How could I be the recipient of his judgment? I do need to understand where he is coming from, that seems the real job at hand.

Gertrude comes over to me as I prepare again to leave for the mission offices. She advises me to look down as he talks and to say nothing. And when he is finished I should just say "thank you" and walk away. I smile at this nutshell teaching on African non-resistance and promise her I'll try.

I resolve not to come across as an aggressive American, but to use these women as my models, the way they hold so true to their inherent dignity despite the assaults from all angles over the years. I straighten my spine and knock lightly on the half-open door to the small office. Father Felipe has redone his hair and has changed into a crisply-ironed, white shirt. He sits imperiously before me in his somewhat shabby office with an annotated copy of the email I sent him a month ago in his hands.

I try a polite pleasantry, "Where do you come from in Mexico?" I ask innocently as I take my seat.

"Near Guadalajara. But I wonder, are you an educated woman?"

I am surprised at his authoritative tone and his opening line of attack.

"This letter is not good English. Even I, a non-native English speaker could do better. And look, there is not even a proper heading."

Internally I am shaking my head and thinking, oh no, a rules junkie. I never do well with them. Out loud, I make a move to soothe his ruffled pride, telling him how sorry I am if my letter felt disrespectful. I was simply trying to explain, and I was upset. I wrote fast and it was not meant as an insult to him.

He begins his speech and goes on and on with the ways in which I have broken the rules, not kept records. I just listen, as Gertrude instructed. I am amazed at his angle. Then he starts in on what a failure the Mapusha Cooperative is, and how the Catholic church likes to teach people to fish not give them fish. His implication that they have been sucking off the mission all these years riles me.

Then, despite myself, I go off on him. I suggest he is the one who disrespected the women. He denies it completely and puffs himself up, suggesting we go over and ask the women.

Uh-oh. He has me there. I don't want to get into a power battle between him and the women, I don't want them to be in a position where they might cave out of deference to him as a representative of their church. I decline the offer, but he is provoked. He starts a rant about Regina and Gertrude.

" How can I even talk to this man? I find myself veering into the vulnerable realm as he goes on and on about no records, no paperwork, no rules, no order. I have believed forever that the best way to really get to the bottom of things is to be as vulnerable and honest as possible and I try it.

I explain to him the way people trust in my world. The people who gave support to Mapusha to fix the roof and build a bathroom trusted me, and trusted that the work would get done. We trusted Father Miguel when we made the agreement about the water, and Father Chico about the bathroom. Everyone trusted me and trusted Mapusha.

My eyes fill with tears as I try to impress upon him that our way is the way of trust, the heart. The sinking sensation in my belly begins in earnest. I am tumbling into the paralyzing zone of the powerless, the judged, the wrongdoer, this time it is not me, it is the women of Mapusha whom he judges so harshly. I am unable to protect them and that feels as bad as not being able to protect myself.

He goes on and on. I don't hold what he says as any sort of truth, but I feel myself taking up less and less space in the room. He tells me that the women will grow from giving a contribution monthly to the mission. He keeps using that word, contribution.

"It isn't a contribution," I say in exasperation. "It is rent for a building that has been theirs for 36 years, and it is rent they cannot afford."

He pays me no mind. He is winning the battle. I can't put my finger on how or why but he is. After an hour and a half we shake hands and I depart the confining space. The women are sitting on a bench in the yard, waiting for me. They were worried, they tell me. I try to explain to them how it went, what he thinks, how I cried.

I feel slimed, as though just sitting there with him and his judgments has made me somehow culpable. I should have followed Gertrude's advice to the tee or really had it out with him with loud words and anger, but that isn't how it went. His voice was well modulated, but there was a strange way he bullied me. I cried for them. I shrank for them. I tell Regina I feel as though I disappointed her and she assures me it is not true.

It is a long night of tossing and turning, remembering what he said and how he looked, and trying different answers on for size. I suspect his anger is often aimed at women. His fury at the notion, put into his head by somebody, that they laughed at him, the women of Mapusha laughed at him is the central clue to his fears and his defenses. He aimed for Regina and Gertrude because they are the most empowered of the women at the church.

He told me that when he got my letter all he could say was "Who are you?" He kept repeating that phrase. "Who are you?" His thinking is so outside my realm of reality that I mostly feel puzzled. At one point he told me not to interrupt him for he had an outline to follow. I really don't know what the outline was, but I do know that its purpose was to prove me completely wrong about everything, to point out that I am both powerless and a nobody to boot. And none of that really matters, I don't give a rip what he thinks of me, but he got to me. He managed to tap into that old, too familiar shame of powerlessness.

This isn't my battle. It is theirs. And mostly, it is Regina's. I try to envision the gesture that will most clearly support and empower her?

# A New Way

The next morning as I sit with my coffee on the deck it is clear what I must do, clear as the turquoise water in the pool before me I will call Regina and tell her I will stand with them and support them, but they are the bosses. I will take a back seat to their management of the problem. It is a beautiful, damp morning after a night of rain and spring birdsong fills the early morning air. I let the sounds and the greens of the bush wash through me and know that whatever the women want to do, I am behind them. They lead, and I will stand with them because I trust them and honor their wisdom. I will do what the Father will not.

I call and explain to Regina. She tells me she was awake all night as well. She thanks me for my call and we decide to talk on Tuesday.

Regina and I sit on the bench watching Zanile laughing. She is seated on a cushion that is being pulled in circles by her big sister, Elena. We both remember when it was Elena, not Zanile, who was toddling about the studio. She must have many memories of babies who learned to walk on these smooth floors. I am outraged every time I consider the Father and anxious to hear what Regina has to tell me about their chosen course of action.

I get right to the nut of it, asking about their decision. Now you have had two meetings with him, I have had one meeting with him and we still have that awful signed agreement that Mapusha will pay R800 a month and be evicted in 2014.

She is calm, clear and emphatic.

"We will stay here at Mapusha. We will pay the rent if we have the money after we pay our salaries and we will never pay more than R800. We will go to church, we will care for the church because we love God but we will not be involved in any other way with the

214

mission. We know what is true. We know God. We will stay." She makes a finalizing gesture with both hands.

Okay, I get it. Though it is far from my usual response to things, I understand it. They have chosen to avoid a direct confrontation with the Mission, but to follow a path which allows them their dignity.

"Do the other women agree with this?"

"Yes they do."

She is clear. I smile. Obviously she has moved through this process in her own way. She is forging a path that is true for her and I get it. She is claiming her own right and truth above the word of the head priest at the mission for the first time. It may be a silent resistance but it is a "no", and it will be felt. I take a deep breath, appreciating the magnitude of this decision for Regina.

I climb up onto the bench where Gertrude is weaving. She says the same thing in so many words. She tells me that at church yesterday they wanted her to come to some meeting or other, but she walked home after church instead.

"We want Mapusha to leave the mission, but we have no money so we will stay. It is our building, but everything is different now."

And so our course of action is settled and I tell Gertrude, as I told Regina, that I will do whatever they want. I am the follower, not the leader. Gertrude nods and we both smile. She seems as pleased with this change in positions as I am. I look at the rug she is weaving and ask if it isn't high enough as it is.

"No, we will make one more square," she replies and we both laugh again for she is, again, being the boss.

"Okay."

I do my best to keep my opinions cloaked and follow the lead of the women but the outrages continue. Daily, I push open the door of the studio and glance around at the varied weaving stations, watching for any sign that something has happened. The battle with the mission is in full swing but Anna Mbetsi sits with her paintbrush at a small table draped with her current tablecloth project. Regina is hard at work on the giraffe tapestry that needs to be finished by the end of the week so it can go back to the States in my bag.

On the other side of the room Wonder is talking on the phone. She is speaking English. " I don't think she knows," I hear her say, and I look at her and cock my head. Is she talking about me? If so, what is it that I don't know? Zanile sees me coming in her direction and sets off at a run on her chubby little legs for the safety of her mom. She laughs with delight as she reaches the haven between her mother's knees and reaches her hand up to Ambrocia's breast as though yelling "home free!"

"Is there something I don't know?" I ask Wonder as I sit down at their sewing table.

"Yes, you do not know that they turned our water off."

"What? They turned the water off for the co-op on this hot, hot day?"

"Yes, they turned it off on Monday. We asked the gardener and he said the Father told him because we have not paid our rent to turn the water off for Mapusha. He said if we have a question, come to speak with him."

I speak with Regina about this latest outrage. I vowed I would follow the women's lead, but everything in me wants to go screeching over to the mission, pound on the door and confront him as he deserves to be confronted.

"We are speaking with the executive committee. We will take turns going to fetch water at the high school. Wonder and Ambrocia went yesterday and Gertrude and I will go today."

I consider the irony of it all. When I first came to the studio the mission shared their borehole and pump with the whole community. Women lined up with wheelbarrows and water containers on the lawn. When the mission put a fence around the pump and stopped helping the community with their water needs we asked if we could get a line for water from their borehole to the studio. We needed water for dying the wool and there were always thirsty children about. The Fathers gave us permission in exchange for a donation of $1,000, and he guaranteed the cooperative water rights.

But Father Felipe says that this Father was not right and there are no written records, so our agreement is not real, null, void, did not happen. Often there is no water in the village and their gardens are at the mercy of the skies, but at least at the studio, they could boil water for tea and wash their hands.

Gertrude comes over with two plastic 20-liter water containers in her hand. She and Regina go out the door and I run to get my camera and yell out to them, "I'm coming, too."

Walking behind them through the yard I fantasize about the article I will one day write. I will need pictures. Regina and Gertrude have that certain look about them that I have come to know. They are doing what needs to be done without complaint or fuss. They need water and they will get it. As they let the water from the single tap fill their buckets they chat with some older women who are sitting with their snack wares ready to sell to the high school students as they leave the building.

I can think only one thing, "It isn't right."

She nods in agreement as she rolls one heavy container out from under the spigot and then rolls the second one forwards to be filled. They help each other to get the heavy containers onto their heads and then start their stately walk back to the studio, doing what needs to be done. I follow, snapping pictures.

I continue struggling to understand their decisions. Emerencia becomes my ally, friend and translator. So much is unspoken yet understood by all in the community, as though they are speaking a language of hand gestures. I sense the undercurrent of tacit understanding, but I miss the fine points. Emerencia tells me about jealousies within the church, women who resent the amount of power Regina and Gertrude wield there. Maybe it was these small jealousies which started the problem with the new Father. Maybe he had received wrong information about Regina and Gertrude. It is gratifying for me to watch my feisty young apprentice step up and out into the world. She is not afraid of conflict. Her new job as secretary at the grade school has given her a chance to stretch herself and she is getting comfortable wielding power. She confides that she is going to go to the Women of St. Anna, she thinks they are the ones who will be able to set things straight. This seems right and it is much better that Emerencia use the channels of the church to untangle things, much better than outsider me barging in with my clumsy, sure to cause trouble savior stance. I sit, silent with my chin in my hands. There is nothing to say or do, only watch.

## Peace is More Important than Right?

Two weeks later, we sit in the shade on the new triangular steps of the creche building, Nick, Stephen and I are on the left of Father Keister. Regina, Gertrude and Anna Mduli on his right. We are gathered to hear from this man who was responsible for building these structures ten years ago. We need to know who owns these buildings; the creche, the art center and the Peanut building.

The women have come with him from morning mass and are neat in their shirtwaist dresses and crisp bandanas. Nick has been working on the new community art center, painting and sanding and repainting the blackboards. I have been working for three days to get the creche's front wall painted with a mural honoring the woman whose memorial fund paid for the creche's latest uplift.

Father Keister is obviously at home here in the rural community. He wears sneakers with sensible socks and khaki shorts, a worn cotton shirt. His lean face is wrinkled and his grey hair thinning, but there is vitality and a kindness emanating from his blue eyes and spare frame. He sets a gentle tone, teasing the women to speak, challenging them to participate, chiding them for the curtains that were stolen from the Peanut building. They know, they know where those curtains are, he teases.

Regina protests, "No Father, we do not know who took the curtains." But there is a smile on her face and I know she trusts this Father.

We all listen as he tells us why these buildings were built and why the women from the community are the owners of the property. Somehow I feel as though I am in Sunday school. I listen closely to what the teacher is saying, trying to understand the deeper resonances of his words. Clearly, he loves this community and understands its people. What is central is that he wants to help them help themselves. Empowerment isn't the word he uses, but that is the essence of his words.

There is a buzzing silence as we look out at the new latrine and the old Peanut building, which has stood empty these last ten years. Regina, Gertrude, Anna and Anna plant their peanut and sweet potatoes crops in the fenced yard of the small building. Father Keister himself erected the fence around the it, but he confirms the building is the women's to do with as they choose. They are the board that oversees these community buildings and he is happy to see what is happening here, now. His vision is of a community that can look after and out for itself.

When he challenges the women to make this community center what it could be, I know I must raise the issue of the eviction of the women from their studio of 36 years.

I stumble a bit but won't let myself stop, 'But it is not right what is happening at the mission. The women have been there 36 years. Thousands of dollars of international support have gone into making the building what it is today."

"Yes," he nods "but it would be better for the women to move Mapusha here to that building. He indicates the Peanut building. It will bring peace. We cannot really speak of this. It is not my place."

We all stand to go over to the Peanut building and walking beside him down the dusty path in the hot midday sun I can't help but continue. I want to be heard by a representative of the mission.

"But he disrespects the women of Mapusha. How do I talk to someone like this? It is not very Christian."

Phew, I got it out. The core of my upset is curled around this representative of the church treating people, particularly women, as he does.

Father Keister stops and turns to me. He doesn't actually take my hand but it feels as though he has.

"You may be right, but, your peace is more important."

We continue through the fence of the little building, which the women were originally meant to run as a store. It never worked because when hungry women came with no money they gave them food on credit. The store went broke, but Gertrude and Regina had remained true to their Christian principles of generosity.

I recognize the peace I do suddenly feel. That simple interaction with Father Keister in the field has freed up something. I can breathe fully again for the first time since this began weeks ago.

It is time for Father Keister to go. He will be back in January with his sister, and he will bring the constitution and we will have a community meeting. He strides off and I turn to Stephen and Nick to seek confirmation.

"He really was that wonderful?"

They both nod.

The women of Mapusha are admiring the elephant that is appearing on the welcoming wall of the creche. The mural is of an elephant washing himself in the early, early morning. It feels right, all feels right. To move the studio here could be a new dawn for the women of Mapusha and the community.

Stephen begins measurements at the current Mapusha studio, and then measures at the potential new studio. I feel excitement beginning to bubble. Our plan is to renovate the Peanut building. It will become a new wonderful studio for the cooperative. It will be a building they own as well as being part of the burgeoning community center.

Stephen and Nick talk over his vision for the building He wants to knock out all the interior walls and use the bricks to make a big covered patio at the back of the building. Then he wants to take off the roof and build a higher wall with a pitched roof and have the front porch set up for display.   We stand at the back of the building looking out at the plowed field within the fence, out over the valley of Rooiboklaagte. There is one particularly beautiful tree on the plot and the view is expansive. Stephen is going home to draw up the plans. The women are relieved. They do own these buildings and they have a responsibility to the community. I am beginning to dream of the potentials for this community hub.

## Mapusha Stands Up

I have a date with Eulender, Gertrude's bright grandchild, after the Sunday morning church service at the mission. I am in my usual back pew position, standing with the congregation to sing, only I don't sing. I let their voices wrap and penetrate me. I watch a little girl on her father's shoulder watch me. Stretching to see the front of the church I cannot find a single woman from Mapusha. They wouldn't stay away from church because of the problematic Father, who thankfully isn't here in the mission church today. They must be at one of the endless weekend funerals. Mostly they are the funerals of their friend's children, nieces, nephews, the thirty-something generation. The virus slammed them as they reached sexual maturity about when the virus caught fire in their previously segregated world. The good roads that the Nationalist government constructed were the perfect conduits for the disease. The system of black men working in the cities, leaving their wives behind in the rural villages also assisted with the wildfire spread of the HIV virus.

After the service I see Eulender in the yard. I have raised money from friends in the states for her to attend a private school in Hoedspruit, and she has written a thank-you note for me to give to her supporters. She wears a lacy black shawl over her slim Sunday dress and she giggles like any school girl. She is loved by all in the community and is an inspiration to many. I tell her about the man who says that all children must know they can be change-makers, that they have the power to change the world. I ask if she believes she can change the world?

She doesn't hesitate, "I know I can make a difference."

I hug her slim body and she trips off across the lawn on her high heels to find her friends. I talk more with Regina about the possibility of moving Mapusha over to the Peanut building, raising money to renovate it using Stephen's designs. She needs to talk with the women about this idea, we need to know if the mission is serious about evicting them. She understands well what I am saying and we decide they will meet early in the week, without me. I drive home so caught in my head that it is only when I see an eagle floating not too far above that I stop and see the afternoon light on the green of the mountains and notice the very tips of the grasses on the roadside just turning pale yellow. The peak of the lush summer has passed and the slide begins towards the brown of winter.

My eyes are focused on the bees drinking the salt from the edge of Leslie and Brad's pool, but my mind is swirling with the Mapusha studio. If the women decide to go for the renovation of the Peanut building I will have my work cut out for me fundraising for the building project while I am in the States. There is great appeal to starting them in a new building close to the creche and the new Seeds of Light art center, and away from the mission, but the truth is that only 60% of their too-low salaries came from sales last year, and it was their best year ever. I don't know how they will match or equal sales this year other than by my own major efforts.

Weavings and tapestries are difficult to sell. Tapestries hung on walls in the 80's, but they don't work as well in 2010, I know that in my designer bones, yet somehow, the women have gotten their salary each month for the last nine years. Often Regina has told me that God is with Mapusha and I can only nod my head. I am not good at marketing, but I care immensely, and somehow that, coupled with who the Mapusha women are, has made it work. I am pulled to this world and to their world still.

I admire the pyramid form of the mountain, Modimilo, in front of me which drew Leslie and thus, all of us to this reserve on the Blyde river twelve years ago. I let myself slide in, dip into the clear salted water of the pool. The bees hover or find a bit of leaf to sit on as the water moves over the edge with my entry. The wind is loud in the trees and the human silence is alive. I dive down into the water before a flood of love tears for Africa begins.

In the morning Regina calls out that we will all have a meeting. "We had a meeting yesterday, but we want to have a meeting with you now," she informs me with a new vigor. She is deeply engaged, and I am happy when I remember how sad and confused her eyes were when I first arrived six weeks ago. She has had many sleepless nights over these latest struggles.

She begins by saying they talked long and hard at yesterday's meeting about moving the studio to the Peanut building.

"Some were very excited by the idea but others felt it would cost too much money. We would need security there."

She goes silent and it is clear that someone else must speak. I look around at the women and for once it is a meeting where everyone is fully present.

"We have decided to stay, to fight for our building at the mission." says Gertrude with a nod of her head. "The Peanut building will be the center for the community. We will run it and try to help get skills training for the unemployed women but the Mapusha studio will stay here, where it has always lived."

I go around the circle, looking into the eyes of each of the ten women of the studio. Wonder is obviously on-board with this empowered decision. Anna and Anna are in agreement.

"Is this what you want?" I ask Lindy.

"No metata." No problem, she replies.

The women will move forward with their complaint about the rent and the eviction to the executive board.

## Goodbye Mapusha

Nearing the end of my time with the women of Mapusha, I drink in every sound, smell and sight as I drive through the center of Acornhoek trying not to fret about the unresolved situation with the mission. At the stoplight I take in the woman walking in front of me. White paint streaks her face. Her red and black sarong tells me that she is a Sangoma, a Zulu healer, in training from Swaziland. I will miss the fabric wonderland of this crowded marketplace. I love the way the women combine the four fabrics of their dress———the headscarf, blouse, skirt and sarong. I remember being four-years-old and relishing choosing my own outfits. I remember, too, watching my niece, Claire, delighting in clothing her young body in a patchwork combination of stripes, florals and leopard skin prints. The women here have fun with their fabrics, too, and wear them with grace and dignity. They don't worry about what shape they are. Fat or thin, their main concern is dressing themselves beautifully, and then proudly walking into town.

Turning onto the dirt road, I see the school children in light-blue shirts and dark slacks skipping and frolicking along the road before the first bell of the morning. They wave, giggle and gesture as I pass by. I wave back wildly, knowing I will sorely miss their exuberance.

"We will stay this afternoon at the studio and wait for the executive committee to come and speak with us," says Wonder.

She gives me a play-by-play of their meeting last week with one member of the board. She says Regina opened the meeting. She spoke long and hard about the building, their building. They helped to build the building 36 years ago, they made the bricks. It was built for the poor women by the poor women of the community and the mission has no right to charge them for it.

"She told him we will not pay to use this building. It was built for us. We will pay for water and electricity but not for the building."

I am proud imagining Regina speaking those words. I know her power. Once, years ago, I watched Sampiwe sing a song for the group. She squatted down and sang with a big, strong voice that surprised me coming from such a little girl. I said to Regina, "I bet you had a big voice like Sampiwe when you were small." She chuckled and agreed with me, yes she did once have a big voice and it has emerged once again. I know she brought that big voice out of the closet when she spoke to the committee and I know they heard her.

Wonder goes on telling me about the meeting.

"Then they asked how much Mapusha was willing to pay and Gertrude said R400."

Interesting. That is half of what the mission had demanded, so negotiations are underway. The committee will meet today, and the women will wait to hear what is decided. I sit beside Zanile's cot stroking her head as she naps, deciding whether to wait with the women for the committee's report or whether just to drive back to Blyde and leave them to deal with it themselves. Part of me wants to stay and join the fight. No, I will leave and try to trust that things will go well.

Slowly, slowly I seem to be letting go of my savior stance here at the cooperative. The biblical image of Judith with her sword raised to save the downtrodden is fading. They are standing up for themselves. I flash on that moment years ago when I told Regina she was the boss of the guy working on the roof of the studio. She couldn't fathom the notion that she was the boss of this man but now she has taken on the executive board at the mission.

As I heat my supper I dial Wonder on the landline and watch the fading light through the high triangular window as the phone rings.

"Hello Wonder, How are you?" I have learned that this greeting is not to be forgotten despite my impatience to learn what happened when the executive board came to the co-op this afternoon.

"They didn't come to see us. They had a meeting at the mission, but then they just drove out without coming to see us. We are just leaving now."

It is 5:30, an hour after the women usually leave the cooperative. Angy has an hour's walk ahead of her. Upset moves through me again as I consider how the women have been disrespected once again.

"Will Gertrude call them? Do they know about the water?"

Wonder assures me that she will but I am teaching a yoga retreat this weekend so there is nothing more I can do. The very place where I want to save them is where, in fact, they need to save themselves. How can I think that my power could be a substitute for theirs? It is arrogance. There truly is nothing I can do to help them with this. My job is to prepare to drive to White River for my retreat in the bush with my yoga buddy, Jean. Yoga and silence with seven South African women while the women of Mapusha continue their fight alone.

## Resolution at Sabi Sand

I stand on the deck of Jean's family compound in the Sabi Sands Reserve, basking in the fragrant bush surrounding me, the huge fig tree's fruit-filled branches spread high above me, wider than my eyes can hold. We have just completed the yoga retreat and it went well. The seven women looked radiant and relaxed when they left. I let myself sink into the big, round, cushioned chair and swivel to face the all-encompassing tree. I'm grateful to be in the midst of such beauty and aware that in the moment my most faithful, balanced center of self is at the wheel.

There is movement above me. I catch sight of a small dark head with shiny inquisitive eyes. Long, thin fingers are reaching out for a yellow fig bud. The more I watch the more of them I see. A large vervet monkey troop have come on an afternoon fig raid. Gradually they relax in my presence and start up their little squawks and squabbles. There are many babies and they aren't tucked on their mother's bellies as is the way with baboons. These babies are free to explore the tree and its fruits on their own. One little guy reaches up for a branch and loses his balance while two others get very still as they witness their friend stumble. He finds his way back up and they recommence with their branch exploration.

It seems an easy metaphor for what is happening with the women of Mapusha, but in fact they aren't stumbling up a learning curve in this confrontation with the mission. It is more a Clark Kent, finally exposing their Superwomen side. They have dropped their submissive disguise. They are daring to stand in their inherent power.

Fifty years ago, pigtailed Gertrude and Regina attended the new Catholic mission school for instruction on what is right and what is wrong. I laugh considering the irony in their current actions. Now they are using these very lessons to defend themselves from the institution that taught them. And there is irony, too, in how well the Father's of the church have served the co-op. They were an instrument of empowerment; unwittingly they gave the women a challenge big enough that they were forced to speak up.

I consider my relationship with David and Leslie, how conflict with these two heroes of mine is what helped set me free. In both relationships, the hurts which had seemed so deep and insoluble were swallowed by the larger flow of love. It had taken work to understand and untangle my varied disappointments. As I listen to the squabbling monkeys on a branch above my head, I see my willingness to stand in conflict with these two gave me the power to move from seeing them as giants to a more equal playing field of mutual respect and cooperation. It is simple now to choose love.

When I returned to South Africa and went to the farm for a visit with David and Neil, I was welcomed with open arms. As we sat on the couch exchanging news and ideas I enjoyed the same ease and delight of our past relationship but I could also sense a new breath of detachment. In my relationship with Leslie, a similar change occurred. One hot Sunday afternoon, at my instigation, we met at a Women of St. Anna celebration. We hugged each other surrounded by a dancing, singing crowd of Sunday-dressed women and all the wrinkles of past hurts seemed smoothed away. I knew we had morphed into the possibility of a more grown-up relationship; I had worked to untangle and release my child-like sense of a fairy god-mother and weathered the loss. On that sunny day we danced together and then as we stood outside with the summer sun beating down, we talked of the first visit to Africa I took with her and all the actions which had been birthed by the 1998 tour.

It was just as Father Keister had shown me, right and wrong pale beside the deeper harmony of peace. Both conflict and letting-go were important steps in the healing process leading to the deeper reality of love in my friendships. I sigh with gratitude and know that the women of Mapusha will emerge from their own conflict with the mission more empowered, and less dependent on the outside world to dictate their truth.

The breeze stirs the leaves of the tree and my eyes soften, letting boundaries dissolve. I merge with the dance of the leaves with the sky and the shifting sparkles of the sun. I can see the ways I have moved with the women of Mapusha over the years. It all feels perfectly right. We came together when we were both in need of support, we weathered the collapse of our old ways and stumbled together in a new direction. We found each other, joined forces and here we are today, ten years later.

I remember Wonder's words last year. "Judy, you don't know this, but we all think of you as our mother, even Regina." I was shocked because, in my own way, I felt as though these women were my mothers. I became a mother to eleven African women and they became mothers to me. Mother love, this immense caring which formed the basis of our relationship, grew and grew to include so many people - the children of the creche, the art class kids, the grade school learners, Tiyiselani and the hundreds of people from the U.S. and Europe, Brazil and Canada who visited, supported and cheered for all of us.

My eyes rest on the clouds moving fast across the wide blue African sky and I consider how much more love, trust and hope came into the world through my time with Mapusha. I feel a deep and welcome joy. Jean comes out looking as happy and tired as I feel and we set off with our bags and bundles in her car for White River. As we drive in companionable silence out of the reserve I continue to muse on the beauty of this dance between Mapusha and me, and leaving the magical bush behind, I wonder what the next steps will bring.

# Epilogue

## FLYING HIGH

# Another Plan, Another Studio

I planned to end my story here, to settle back into Portland and write it all down with the hope of inspiring others to take a leap of faith and get out there to make a difference. That is not the way it goes.

On my way back to Portland I visit Dahlia in her friendly home up the Hudson River from the big city. It seems a fitting segue between South Africa and Portland. Dahlia is the perfect person to help me adjust to a transition once again. We will go to the farmers' market and climb into the hills of Minnewaska, eat lettuce and strawberries from her garden, and venture out in the motorboat with her husband, Lee, at dusk, listening to his favorite '60s rock music as the sun sets.

My cell rings as we stand in front of a strawberry stand at the New Paltz farmer's market. It is Jodi, a friend from Alaska, with news that she says I must sit down to hear. Obligingly, I find a packing crate in a quiet corner and sit. Jodi is a dynamo healer from Homer, Alaska who has led trips all over the world to help women and children. She has twice been to South Africa with her group of good-hearted healers, and her support for Mapusha has been stupendous for years. I'm tingling with curiosity as she begins to explain.

A friend wants to donate forty thousand dollars to a project in South Africa, and she has chosen Mapusha from among Jodi's many projects. She wants them to have a new studio, to be free of what she perceives as the Catholic mission's tyranny. It literally takes my breath away. Can it be true?

It is true.

All thoughts of weaning myself from the Rooibok world disappear. The Portland plan splatters to earth and evaporates. Someone has to manage this project, and there is no one to do it but me————who hates hardware stores! It is unimaginable that I could be a project manager for a building crew erecting a large building in Rooiboklaagte. But then, at one time so was the idea that I could help sustain and uplift a woman's weaving coop in rural South Africa. I believe that where there is a will and heart and humility there is almost always a way, but my eyes widen to imagine this, my new job.

I am back in South Africa in January of 2013, as ready to begin as I ever will be. The studio is to be built on the New Dawn Center's property, which Father Keister long ago staked out for the community. He made the Mapusha women the trustees of the land parcel, the three buildings and two large semi-fenced plots. It is as though twenty years and Father Felipe's egregious acts have joined forces to make everything roll out just as Father Keister envisioned.

The studio will grow the New Dawn Center. The weaving studio will join Katlego Creche and the Seeds of Light Art Center around the central lapa. All will share the borehole abundance and mural decorated outhouses. We dream that one day the Peanut building will become a community learning center. Soon the douser will come to find the perfect spot to try digging a well, which will provide us with water for all to drink and cook and wash. There will be gardens. Already the Mapusha women put on their garden shoes when it is lunchtime and walk over to New Dawn to prepare the soil. My nephew and his new wife have raised wedding funds for a play structure for the kids, and I am envisioning a good fence to keep the goats and cows out.

The Mapusha women are about to assume their rightful place as the stewards of a Rooiboklaagte community center. Regina takes it in stride, more proof that the God she so loves does indeed love Mapusha and hear their daily prayers. Peace has been restored at the mission and Father Felipe is now friendly with Regina and Gertrude. Emerencia appealed to the Women of St. Anna, and a meeting was arranged. It was all a misunderstanding and he apologized to them.

If Regina's experience with the mission was her true coming of age experience, the seven months I spend project managing the building of this new studio is mine. I am thrown into a new world of men and hardware stores, procuring items for the building crew that I don't understand in the least, and wrestling with sub-contractors, water supply and delivery trucks.

I have a major confrontation with the donor's husband on a rainy day, which happens to be my 62nd birthday. He doesn't like my style, my propensity to trust. They both feel Kevin's design centered on three central arches is a grand extravagance. They want a time-line and budget projections from Kevin. I am passionately against losing the arches and unwilling to ask Kevin, the architect who is working pro-bono, to spend two days penning projections. It is a face-to-face confrontation on the New Dawn central lapa.

He stands over me, red-faced and shaking his finger in my face, and I bristle and yell back, among other things, "You are a bully." It is unpleasant and the final note comes when the donor herself hisses, "Not another penny for this project."

The silver lining, other than my refusal to shrink or silence any part of myself, comes when I see out of the corner of my eye the way all the workers have stopped in their tracks and are silently but tangibly supporting me as they watch our confrontation. They stand with me against this man who looks and feels so like their old oppressors. It shows me how completely the community has claimed me as one of their own. The donors leave with none of their demands answered, and I know I will be fund raising again to complete the studio. So be it.

The money is raised and I fight my way to hardware store sufficiency and spread sheet mini-mastery. I beg help daily from Nick and listen hard to the advice of many, and the studio moves inexorably forward towards completion.

Watching Gertrude and Regina gaze up at the completed arches before the roof is in place makes me cheer. It is like a church, they conclude with big smiles. Then there is the sunny Sunday when I sit wide-eyed on the lapa looking up at Jack's roofing crew, barefoot and high, high up on the thin beams, nailing the big sheets of tin into place. And I see the joy brought to the community kids by the new play structure with its slides and ladders. Just watching the kids play easily erases the memory of 100 tedious trips to the hardware stores. I will hold tight to the image of Elena's smile when she soars high in a swing for the very first time.

I did it. We did it. We set the date for our opening blessing celebration in early August.

## Celebration

Today is the official opening of the new studio. Standing before the mirror in my old rondavel at the Blyde Reserve I consider the ceremony as I brush my teeth. Nick and Vicki will be my stalwarts today as they have been throughout this building project, and Jean will come up from White River to stand at my side. There will be a good number of friends from Hoedspruit and Desmond, the foreman, his workers and their families, the Fathers from the mission and all of the Mapusha and Tiyiselani women with their families. It will be a good mix of white and black, well-off and just-getting-by. I smile to think of the rainbow of children who will be swinging and sliding and climbing on our bright new play structure. Bringing my thoughts to the studio itself I give a silent cheer for Kevin and his design, which is both simple and elegant.

We spent yesterday sweeping and cleaning, setting up displays of the women's weavings, buying kilos of meat to brai. The studio is beautiful with its shiny tin roof and rough white walls. The curved bench on the covered porch by the front door is welcoming. I can imagine, in days to come, the spinners setting up their work station here, greeting the creche kids walking by on the way to the outhouse, or welcoming the art class grade-school children coming by to get a drink of water from the sink. Gardens are flourishing with the new fences and the wonder of our functioning borehole. The Mapusha studio makes the New Dawn Center a living, breathing, functioning community center. Amazing.

As I let the water run in the sink, I imagine walking into the studio for the first time, as many will today. The three arches dividing the space are the real heart of the building. They give it a sense of grace. Rugs woven by Gertrude, Lizbeth and Angy hang on rods framed by the rough white walls. On the far side of the large space each of the floor-looms has a special nook and shelf for displaying the work of the weaver. The work in each is beautiful in its own unique way. Regina has one tapestry in flowing greens that

I know will impress the art gallery owners. They will be at the celebration, and will marvel at the charm of Lindy's small cotton tapestry of a buffalo sniffing an extravagant purple flower, or the one with a mother zebra nuzzling her baby under the tree. We have done well, this 40-year-old women's weaving cooperative and me.

Cupping hot water in my hands and throwing it on my face with eyes closed I picture the motto painted on the sign for the New Dawn Center. "Together we have strength." I will use these words as the center of my talk at the gathering today. Working here with the women in their village has taught me this lesson on two levels. I have watched support pour into the village of Rooibok from all over the world, inspiring hope and creating opportunity for so many. On a personal level I understand the power of people joining forces from my relationship with the women of Mapusha.

Yesterday, at the end of the day, when our preparations were complete and the studio was being carefully locked up for the night, I stood with Regina on the porch. I handed her the keys to the studio, and for an instant our eyes met. All the subtle barriers between us dropped away and we both simply nodded. She put the keys in her pocket and patted them with a smile.

Truly, there is cause for celebration today. I pull my long hair up and clip it in my usual haphazard style. I recall a penciled self-portrait from way back in the 80's with this same hair-style. These days my face is lined and sun-spotted, my clipped up pile of hair is streaked with grey, yet the same green eyes gaze back at me. I'm reminded of that chemo-induced mirror moment, the bald woman whose eyes were filled with such shame and helplessness. Today, there is not a hint of either in the eyes looking back at me. Musing on the gradual healing of that hidden hurt of mine, I see it was my concern for the women of Mapusha that inspired me time and again to stand up and speak out. The act of speaking broke through those ghost-ridden, fear-filled barriers of silence and shame. Regina, too, has learned to speak her truth and neither of us is looking for others to show us the way anymore. There is a sparkle to all of me today and the saucy spiral of hair on top of my head feels just right.

# My thanks!

Thank you seems too mundane a word for all the help I have received in the process of writing this book. It was Dahlia Bartz Cabe who first urged me to write my story and she has been at my side every step of the way. Her home is filled with Mapusha rugs. My brother, Stephen Baker, promised four years ago to stand by me until it was complete and he has done just that with all his skill, caring and humor. Without him this book wouldn't be. He was an email away on the other side of the country but here in Portland it was my sister, Sarah Schmidt and her husband who put up with me daily and watched me twist and turn with the words process. My Writing Friday buddies and my clubhouse of best friends——Gail and Hilary and Patty——kept me standing up and facing forward which was not always an easy task. And finally Patsy Helmetag came galloping to my rescue on the editing front.

My support crowd in South Africa was extensive and I couldn't have been there without David and Neil, Brad and Leslie, Vicki and Johnny, Becky, Jean, Nick and Helene. They all generously were and still are always helping in one way or another.

Of course, it is to the Women of Mapusha and their extended families that I owe the deepest gratitude for without them none of the last twelve magical years would have been as they were.

As is painted on the sign of the New Dawn Center, "Together We Have Power" and in a strange way the very solitary process of writing made me honor even more completely the need for community and the power of working together. I wrote this book to inspire people and to instill hope. I tried to simply tell my tale of how very much happened when many people joined forces. May this book nourish your hope and inspire you both to vision and to action.

**"Action without vision is only passing time, vision without action is merely daydreaming, but vision with action can change the world"**

Nelson Mandela

Judith Baker Miller currently lives in Portland, Oregon trying not to dream of the big sunny sky of South Africa. She is a life coach, a writer and a speaker and continues to do everything she can to support the women of the Mapusha Weaving Cooperative. She will be leading a tour to meet the weavers in November 2016.
judithbmiller.com
mapusha.co.za